a–z of inter-age

D1460094

Professional Keywords series

Every field of practice has its own methods, terminology, conceptual debates and landmark publications. The *Professional Keywords* series expertly structures this material into easy-reference A to Z format. Focusing on the ideas and themes that shape the field, and informed by the latest research, these books are designed both to guide the student reader and to refresh practitioners' thinking and understanding.

Available now

Mark Doel and Timothy B. Kelly: *A–Z of Groups & Groupwork*
Jon Glasby and Helen Dickinson: *A–Z of Inter-agency Working*
Richard Hugman: *A–Z of Professional Ethics*
Glenn Laverack: *A–Z of Health Promotion*
Neil McKeganey: *A–Z of Addiction and Substance Misuse*
Steve Nolan and Margaret Holloway: *A–Z of Spirituality*
Marian Roberts: *A–Z of Mediation*

Available soon

Jane Dalrymple: *A–Z of Advocacy*
David Shemmings, Yvonne Shemmings and David Wilkins:
  A–Z of Attachment Theory
Jeffrey Longhofer: *A–Z of Psychodynamic Practice*
David Garnett: *A–Z of Housing*
Fiona Timmins: *A–Z of Reflective Practice*

a–z of
inter-agency working

Jon Glasby & Helen Dickinson

palgrave
macmillan

First published 2014 by
PALGRAVE MACMILLAN

Palgrave Macmillan in the UK is an imprint of Macmillan Publishers Limited, registered in England, company number 785998, of Houndmills, Basingstoke, Hampshire RG21 6XS.

Palgrave Macmillan in the US is a division of St Martin's Press LLC, 175 Fifth Avenue, New York, NY 10010.

Palgrave Macmillan is the global academic imprint of the above companies and has companies and representatives throughout the world.

Palgrave® and Macmillan® are registered trademarks in the United States, the United Kingdom, Europe and other countries

ISBN: 978–1–137–00532–8

This book is printed on paper suitable for recycling and made from fully managed and sustained forest sources. Logging, pulping and manufacturing processes are expected to conform to the environmental regulations of the country of origin.

A catalogue record for this book is available from the British Library.

A catalog record for this book is available from the Library of Congress.

Printed in China

contents

acknowledgements

The author and publisher would like to thank the following publishers and organizations for permission to reproduce copyright material:

Academy of Management for Figure 1 from Marks, M. and Mirvis, P. (2001) 'Making Mergers and Acquisitions Work: Strategic and Psychological Preparation', *Academy of Management Executive*, 15: pp. 80–94

Blackwell Publishers Ltd for Table 1 from Lowndes, V. and Skelcher, C. (1998) 'The Dynamics of Multi-organizational Partnerships: An Analysis of Changing Modes of Governance', *Public Administration*, 76: pp. 313–333

Palgrave Macmillan Ltd for Table 2 from Sullivan, H. and Skelcher, C. (2002) *Working across Boundaries: Collaboration in Public Services*, p. 39

how to use this book

Anyone working, or intending to work, in health and social care, whether in a professional, management or policy role, will need to understand some of the key policies, concepts and issues surrounding inter-agency working. Written as part of Palgrave Macmillan's *a–z* series, this book provides an overview of key terms and themes likely to be encountered by students and practitioners across the range of disciplines and interests encompassed by the health and social care field.

Our list of entries includes:

- **the key health and social care service user groups**, although language sometimes varies between services, we have focused on children and young people, people with physical disabilities, people with long-term conditions, people with learning difficulties, people with mental health problems, older people and carers.
- **key areas of the system**, including primary care, community services, intermediate care, acute care, public health, social care and local government.
- **key themes within health and social care**, such as personalization, safeguarding, commissioning and delayed hospital discharges.
- **broader themes that influence the delivery of health and social care,** such as markets, governance, evaluation of outcomes, leadership, culture and values.

Although it is possible to read this book sequentially from A through to Z, we expect many readers will want to dip in and out – using the book as a resource as and when a specific theme or issue comes up. With this in mind, we have written each entry in stand-alone fashion but have also included as much signposting and cross-referencing as possible to enable readers to navigate a potentially complex series of topics quickly. The four elements of the book's cross-referencing system are:

1. the contents list, where each of the 'keywords' singled out for discussion in the book is listed in alphabetical order of appearance;
2. 'see also' lists at the start of each entry, which offer suggestions for what you might be interested to read next;
3. italicized cross-references embedded in the narrative. These highlight all the terms which have an entry in their own right in the book on first mention in a given entry;
4. the index – an important supplement to the book's a-to-z structure as not all the ideas contained within these pages could have entries in their own right.

Wherever possible, we have tried to identify a single substantive entry and then cross-refer key terms. For example, *hospital discharge* covers alternative terms such as *delayed transfers* or *delayed discharges*, while *theory* covers a number of key theoretical perspectives. In the same way, the many different terms for joint working are all included under *partnership working*. For readers completely new to this field, this entry is a good starting point for reading, along with the entries on *co-production* and *theory*.

Some of the people reading this book will be practitioners using it as a source of reference when a particular topic crops up at work (e.g. issues such as *hospital discharge* or *safeguarding*). For health and social care students who are relatively new to inter-professional working, it might be helpful to read initial entries on different sectors of the system (*primary care, acute care, community services*, etc.) as well as on specific user groups (*children and young people, older people*, etc.). We hope this will give you an introduction to the way that health and *social care* services work and some of the main client groups. We expect students further through their training to use the book as more of an ongoing resource in much the same way as qualified practitioners.

With these various purposes and needs in mind, we have endeavoured to make each entry short enough to give a concise introduction while offering key sources for further reading for those wanting to explore specific issues in greater detail. We have also flagged recommendations for policy and practice in each entry for those interested in the practical implications of the material. Wherever possible, we have tried to concentrate on key debates from health and social care but we have set these debates in a wider context too by drawing on insights from broader theory and from the public policy and public management literature more generally.

Any book on health and social care struggles with the fact that organizational structures evolve on a regular basis. We have tried to include some of the most recent changes as part of relevant entries so that people new to the topic get not only a sense of the history of particular debates and policies but also a summary of key issues in the here and now. While some of our entries focus on particular English structures, we have also tried to provide more of a UK-wide overview, with a section on *devolution* and on some of the key agendas/policies being pursued in each of the four countries of the United Kingdom.

introduction

Following the Health and Social Act of 2012, the issues of inter-agency working, collaboration and integrated care have become central to national policy and to local practice. As society ages, money gets tighter and public expectations rise, doing things as single professions or agencies is no longer going to be possible – if it ever was. Against this backdrop, practitioners and managers of the future are going to have to work with others in new ways – and this book is designed as a resource to help them.

Unfortunately, it can sometimes be difficult to find good books and helpful material on joint working. All too often, it is not uncommon for health and *social care* students to read books written by someone from the same professional background. Thus, doctors will often read books written by fellow doctors, while nurses will read material by other nurses and social workers will read material by social workers. While this has a clear advantage in being able to help develop and strengthen individual professions, it can also cause problems if the material in question is too focused on a single professional perspective.

Over time, health and social services across the United Kingdom have been developing an increasingly inter-agency and inter-professional focus, recognizing that people do not necessarily live their lives according to the categories we create in our welfare structures. Perhaps best summed up by New Labour's (1997–2010) mantra of 'joined-up solutions to joined-up problems', there have been a series of policies over time to encourage individual practitioners and local organizations to work together more effectively across agency boundaries. Despite a new government in 2010, the emphasis on 'integrated care' has continued – and probably even increased (see, for example, NHS Future Forum, 2012).

As a result, we have designed this a–z guide for people from both health and social care, and for those with an interest in different parts of the system. It is also aimed at readers who may be health and social care students, practitioners, managers or policy makers. Writing for such a diverse audience is never easy – but there are real advantages in adopting more of a whole system, cross-cutting approach. Although we have historically trained different professions in relative isolation from each other, the challenges we face in the current financial and policy context are such that only a joined-up response will suffice. This will require much greater familiarity with each other's worlds and roles, and much greater sharing of perspectives, *values*, contributions and expertise. We hope that this book is a helpful contribution to this agenda.

For a more in-depth discussion of the key issues in *inter-agency working* in health and social care, see:

- Barrett, G., Sellman, D. and Thomas, J. (eds) (2005) *Interprofessional Working in Health and Social Care: Professional Perspectives* (Basingstoke: Palgrave Macmillan)
- Crawford, K. (2011) *Interprofessional Collaboration in Social Work Practice* (London: Sage)
- Glasby, J. (2012) *Understanding Health and Social Care.* 2nd edn (Bristol: The Policy Press)
- Glasby, J. and Dickinson, H. (2008) *Partnership Working in Health and Social Care* (Bristol: The Policy Press)
- Leathard, A. (ed.) (2003) *Interprofessional Collaboration* (Hove: Brunner-Routledge)

Palgrave Macmillan have also published an *Interagency Working in Health and Social Care* series, with books on

- children's services (Mary Kellett),
- disability (John Swain and Sally French),
- learning disability (Val Williams),
- public health and well-being (Rob Baggott).

a

accountability

SEE ALSO elected members; governance; involvement; local government

When we read newspapers or watch television, many of the news stories that we come across are underpinned by discussions of responsibility and accountability. When a national (or local) football team loses a game, we ask who is accountable for this – is it a single player, the team, the manager or the owner of the club? When there is a serious failing in the care of an individual or a group of service users, is this the fault of an errant individual or team, or is this caused by the fault of the wider organization or even the health and social care system that professionals and organizations operate within? Thus, the issue of the accountability is an important one, which is at the heart of many of our conversations about the everyday world.

Tony Giddens argues that 'to be accountable for one's activities is to explicate the reasons for them and supply the normative grounds whereby they may be justified' (Giddens, 1984, p. 30). At the crux of this definition is the idea that accountability involves holding individuals and organizations responsible for their specific actions and their performance against some predetermined standards of performance. Clearly then accountability is a multi-faceted concept when applied to inter-agency settings. Issues of accountability can be a major barrier to close inter-agency relationships and conversely clear lines of accountability may be a facilitator of collaboration.

Within a context of public services, the range of accountabilities are arguably more complex than in commercial sector organizations, given that they are public bodies and so have a range of purposes rather than simply paying attention to the financial bottom line (Hoggett, 2006). Accountability is therefore a tricky concept and may operate at different levels. At a micro-level, individuals have accountabilities to: the individual service users that they are working with; the *team* they work within; the organization or agency they work for; the professional group that they are part of; and also the wider community and the population at large. This is an extensive array of accountabilities and by itself is not exhaustive of the complete complex patchwork. In relation to service delivery, Mansfield (1982, p. 61) argues that there are four main questions of performance: 'for what (purposes are the services intended), to whom (are the services delivered), when (are the services delivered), and by what means (are the services delivered)?'

Accountability in inter-agency settings can be even more complex as there are likely to be a number of additional factors in play. For example, if a social worker is employed within a *Care Trust* (an NHS (National Health Service) organization), they may feel that their professional accountabilities are under attack or are sidelined as they are within an NHS organization. Or potentially another outcome might be that this individual feels that they need to make themselves even more accountable to their profession as they are within a minority within the organization. Similarly if an individual is asked to sit on a partnership board, they may not be sure whether they are there to represent their profession, their organization or even potentially an interest group that they have a relationship with. These sorts of questions of accountability certainly posed challenges in Brodie's (2004) account of being a service user on a partnership board where it was at times unclear if she was there to represent the voice of service users or as a senior leader of the mental health trust in question. For these reasons, being clear about the 'multiple hats' that individuals wear is important. For such individuals in these circumstances, it may also help them to be explicit with others which 'hat' they are wearing at any one time.

The final point to make in relation to accountability is in relation to that of action. As noted above, one facet of accountability involves holding individuals responsible for performance. Many inter-agency initiatives are often set up with quite broad remits in response to complex, deep-seated social issues (e.g. *area-based initiatives*). It has been argued that public services only have the time and effort to expend on issues that they are formally held responsible for (Bevan and Hood, 2006). As such, collaborative initiatives that have rather abstract aims around improving health inequalities or improving outcomes in a general sense may not be able to drive performance in a way that more specific responsibility for particular services or client groups might.

Recommendations for policy and practice
- Accountability is a complex and multi-faceted complex and in inter-agency settings many different types of accountabilities will be present.
- Clear lines of accountability can be a facilitator of closer inter-agency working and lack of understanding about how accountability functions can cause difficulties in collaborative endeavours. Therefore, helping individuals and groups to be clear about their accountabilities in different contexts can be helpful.
- On an individual level, it can be a useful exercise for practitioners to ask themselves to whom they feel accountable – making a list of the different accountabilities people have under different circumstances can be very revealing.
- Giving inter-agency groupings specific targets and holding them to account for this performance might be a more helpful way to prompt action than more abstract notions of performance.

KEY TEXTS
- Brodie, D. (2004) 'Partnership Working: A Service User Perspective' in J. Glasby and E. Peck (eds), *Care Trusts: Partnership Working in Action* (Abingdon: Radcliffe Medical Press)

  This chapter is an account of a service user who is asked to sit on a partnership board and the complexities that arise from this in terms of accountabilities.
- Hoggett, P. (2006) 'Conflict, Ambivalence, and the Contested Purpose of Public Organizations', *Human Relations*, 59: pp. 175–194

  This paper provides a helpful insight into the complex patchwork of accountabilities that public sector organizations work with.

acute care

SEE ALSO **commissioning; community services; Foundation Trusts; hospital discharge**

In the United Kingdom (as in most developed countries), the health care system is dominated by acute care. This is partly because many health systems were initially set up to provide episodic care in a crisis, treating the individual and (if possible) returning them to full health. With demographic changes, this model no longer feels in keeping with the changing nature of disease – and most users of health services are (often older) people with a number of *long-term conditions* or chronic diseases. Such people may need a hospital in an emergency, but the bulk of their care and support is based around self-care and around back-up support at home and in the community. Arguably, this shift requires a very different mindset and service configuration.

Part of the difficulty in making this shift arises from the central role that hospitals play in our health care system as big, powerful, well-resourced and complex organizations with lots of specialist equipment and highly trained staff. They are also a visible symbol of the NHS itself, and often tend to be very popular with local people. Any attempt to change services (even if it is motivated by a desire to improve outcomes) is therefore instinctively viewed as a cut and as a threat to people's health. If there is even a mention of closing a ward or a unit to reinvest elsewhere, there can be an instant campaign by the media, politicians and local people – making significant change very challenging indeed.

In practice, the notion of 'acute care' is more complex than it may at first appear – with a range of services from local, community or 'cottage' hospitals, to busy District General Hospitals and more specialist tertiary centres providing services on a regional or even national basis. Often, the range of services locally is based on historical patterns, and the overall system does not always feel very planned or fit for purpose given broader demographic, social and technological changes. With major financial challenges in the NHS, some estimates suggest that around 40 hospitals in England may have to close or change radically – or that politicians may need to find an extra £8 billion if they are not prepared to take these significant steps (Corrigan and Mitchell, 2011). There is also a series of reviews underway to ensure that a range of very specialist services (e.g. children's heart surgery) can be provided in a smaller number of specialist centres, thus concentrating scarce skills and resources in centres of excellence that should be even safer and higher quality than previous approaches (see, for example, NHS Specialised Services (2010)). However, this is a complex political territory and there are likely to be lots of legal challenges, protests and debate before the configuration of services can change in a meaningful way.

In England, the market reforms of the Thatcher governments transformed hospitals into more standalone 'Trusts', run on a model borrowed from the commercial sector with a board of Executive and Non-Executive Directors. Over time, the power and autonomy of NHS Trusts has increased with the award of 'Foundation Trust' (FT) status to high-performing, financially robust hospitals. More arms-length from the Department of Health than non-FTs, these hospitals have greater financial freedoms and are perhaps more commercially minded. However, to prevent a backbench rebellion, the New Labour government that introduced FT status gave these hospitals something of a 'mutual' feel, with patients and the public able to become 'members' of the Trust and a Council of Governors elected from patients, staff and local people. In practice, FT status coupled with payment systems designed to tackle long waiting times have run the risk of increasing the power of hospitals and sucking care in rather than encouraging a shift to more community-based settings. More recently, *community health services* have been taken away from former Primary Care Trusts (PCTs), and many have merged into larger acute Trusts – thus not only giving scope for a more joined-up approach but also increasing the risk of acute care dominance. It is also unclear what impact new *Clinical Commissioning Groups* (CCGs) will have, and whether these 'CCGs' will have more success than previous *commissioning* bodies in changing the role and structure of acute care.

Recommendations for policy and practice

- Services have historically been geared towards acute, episodic care, and this may no longer be the best model in an era of long-term conditions.
- Hospitals are the most visible and often the most popular institutions of the NHS – and reconfiguring services takes political commitment, courage and skill.
- In England, the granting of FT status and policies to tackle waiting times have arguably given hospitals more power and encouraged them to take on more work, rather than shifting care into the community.
- For some specialist services, provision may be safer if provided in a smaller number of centres rather than spreading scarce skills and resource too thinly – but this is controversial.

- In a difficult financial context, hospitals represent a significant proportion of NHS spending and will be a key part of trying to achieve substantial financial savings. Judging on past history, achieving these savings in practice will be complex and politically difficult.

KEY TEXTS

- Corrigan, P. and Mitchell, C. (2011) *The Hospital Is Dead, Long Live the Hospital* (London: Reform)

  Policy paper exploring future of hospital services, co-authored by a former health government health advisor.

- Fulop, N. *et al.* (2011) 'Implementing Changes to Hospital Services: Factors Influencing the Process and "Results" of Reconfiguration', *Health Policy*, 104 (2): pp. 128–135
- Imison, C. (2011) *Reconfiguring Hospital Services* (London: King's Fund)

  Policy briefing from a leading NHS think tank on the opportunities and barriers concerning acute care reconfiguration.

adult protection

SEE **safeguarding**

area-based initiatives

SEE ALSO **evaluation; Health and Well-Being Boards; mergers and acquisitions; networks**

Although many UK welfare services operate on a single depart-ment basis (e.g. the Department of Health focuses primarily on health care), there has been growing recognition over time that many welfare issues interact. Thus, some very disadvantaged communities might experience greater crime and anti-social behaviour than other areas, have poor access to health care and to education and experience higher unemployment – all at the same time. In response, a number of policies over time have encouraged local services to work together across traditional agency bounda-ries (including with local *voluntary* and community services and with local residents and communities). These have had different names and a slightly different focus, but are often described as 'area-based initiatives' or 'zonal' approaches. Examples include the following:

- **The Children's Fund:** a national programme established in 2000 to prevent social exclusion in children and young people aged 5–13 across 150 local authorities in England (Edwards *et al.*, 2006).
- **Health Action Zones:** an early policy from the New Labour government (1997–2010) to tackle health inequalities, focusing on a series of cross-cutting initiatives in 26 deprived areas across England (Barnes *et al.*, 2005).
- **New Deal for Communities:** New Labour programme to tackle deprivation in 39 communities with some £2 billion investment over a ten-year period (Department for Communities and Local Government, 2010).
- **Sure Start:** cross-cutting New Labour programme to reduce child poverty (Belsky *et al.*, 2007).

For those interested in the *evaluation* and *theoretical* challenges behind understanding the impact of such complex programmes, many of these evaluations drew on *theory-led* rather than *method-led* approaches (explored in a separate entry).

At different times, central government has also sought to encourage greater joint working at local level through a system of local area agreements (also known as LAAs) and local strategic partnerships (also known as LSPs). While national evaluations of these initiatives (see, for example, Department for Communities and Local Government, 2011) have shed additional light on the barriers and success factors to joint working, key concerns were often that centrally mandated targets could take precedence over and crowd out more genuinely local outcomes in the case of LAAs, and that LSPs could become perceived as 'talking shops' if the agencies involved were so tightly performance managed against single agency targets that there was little scope for genuinely whole systems working. Following the Health and Social Care Act 2012, there may be lessons from previous area-based initiatives for new *Health and Well-Being Boards*.

Recommendations for policy and practice
- Focusing on a local area can help to produce a long-term and co-ordinated approach to complex social problems – certainly,

trying to resolve complex issues such as health inequalities without a long-term, joined-up strategy seems doomed to failure.

- At the same time, designating improvement 'zones' runs the risk of further stigmatizing areas that are already struggling, and can lead to something of a competition where each area has to compete to argue that it is the most deprived to try to win funding.
- Although health and social care are key features of many people's lives, they can often be less important to local communities that other issues (such as families, schools, housing, safety and so on). Genuine area-based working therefore requires much broader partnerships than the health and social care focus of this book.
- Alongside public services, private and voluntary services are also key partners – so area-based initiatives can involve working across a *mixed economy of care* as well as across agency boundaries.
- In addition to the work they do during the life of the project, area-based initiatives need to consider issues of sustainability. In the future, will the area look and feel very different to how it does now, or will the underlying issues be the same?

KEY TEXTS

Key national evaluations of previous area-based initiatives and cross-cutting partnerships include Barnes *et al.* (2005) on Health Action Zones, Belsky *et al.* (2007) on Sure Start, Edwards *et al.* (2006) on the Children's Fund and the Department for Communities and Local Government (2010, 2011) on the New Deal for Communities, Local Area Agreements and Local Strategic Partnerships.

assessment

SEE ALSO **data protection; personalization; safeguarding**

Both health and social care are made up of a number of relatively autonomous professions (including medicine, nursing, social work, occupational therapy and so on). Before care or services can be delivered, these professions and other workers have to carry out an assessment – both to determine whether people's needs qualify for services and to decide how best to meet those needs. Typically, each profession will have slightly different responses and interventions at its disposal, and will assess for different things in different ways. For example, a surgical intervention will require a particular kind of attention focused on particular medical and biological factors, while a nursing assessment may focus more on issues such as personal care, pain, tissue viability, nutrition and so on. An occupational therapy assessment might focus more on equipment or adaptations to help people negotiate the built environment, while a social work assessment might focus more on the needs of the individual in their broader social context.

While this professional focus and specialism is entirely appropriate (who would want to be assessed for a surgical procedure without assessment by a suitably qualified specialist?), it can mean that different parts of the system assess, record information and make decisions in isolation for each other. Where people have complex or multi-faceted needs, there has been a trend over time to promote more joined-up assessment, through a single assessment process for older people and a common assessment framework for children and young people. Although this seems a major step forward, some of our previous attempts to integrate assessment have tended to focus on the forms used, the questions asked and the IT systems that process the information collected. While these are all important, assessment might more helpfully be seen as a social process – a conversation with a purpose – and it may be equally as important to explore different professional cultures and approaches to assessment as to focus on single assessment processes.

More recently, social care in particular seeks to recognize that many service users and patients are experts by experience, and often have significant strengths to contribute and expertise in terms of what works for them. This leads to approaches that try to identify and build on strengths (what people can do for themselves) rather than simply identify problems or deficits. The advent of personal budgets as a part of the broader *personalization* agenda has also led to a greater emphasis on supported self-assessment. Services for *people with learning difficulties* have also been at the forefront of approaches known as 'person-centred planning', which often start by exploring what people would like their life to be like, seeing health and social care as a small part of trying to achieve chosen lifestyles rather than as an end in their own right.

Recommendations for policy and practice

- Some situations call for detailed, single profession assessments – and it is often the need for detailed, technical knowledge that led to the creation of different professions in the first place. In other circumstances, a more joined-up assessment and greater information sharing is important to provide a holistic view of the person's needs.
- Assessment can sometimes be confused with the paperwork and the IT systems that professionals use, but are really more of a social process.
- Different professions focus on different things. As an example, social workers often ask nurses how they find it so easy to ask about people's bowels and bladders, while the nurses say they would feel embarrassed to ask about people's money.
- Irrespective of how assessment is conducted, health and social care have historically had separate data collection requirements and different IT systems – and these are often perceived as major systemic barriers at ground level.
- In an era of personalization, adult social care in particular is developing broader approaches based on supported self-assessment and on person-centred planning.

KEY TEXTS

- Cambridge, P. and Carnaby, S. (eds) (2005) *Person-Centred Planning and Care Management with People with Learning Disabilities* (London: Jessica Kingsley)

  Detailed summary of key policy and practice issues relating to person-centred planning and services for people with learning difficulties.

- Heath, H. and Watson, R. (eds) (2005) *Older People: Assessment for Health and Social Care* (London: Age Concern England)

  Comprehensive Age UK handbook on the assessment of older people in health and social care services.

- Milner, J. and O'Bryne, P. (2009) *Assessment in Social Work*. 3rd edn (Basingstoke: Palgrave Macmillan)

  Key textbook for social workers, including exploration of background theory and of assessment in children's and adult settings.

C

Care Trusts

SEE ALSO **Children's Trusts; commissioning; community services; Health and Social Care Trusts (Northern Ireland); mergers and acquisitions; primary care**

In England, the most integrated health and social organizational structure has historically been the Care Trust. Introduced following *The NHS Plan* of 2000 (Department of Health, 2000), Care Trusts were fully *merged* organizations that were either provider-based (often *mental health trusts* providing health and social care) or PCT-based (i.e. both *commissioning* and providing integrated health and social care). Although ministers initially claimed that all services for *older people* would be provided by Care Trusts within five years, this did not come to fruition – with a maximum of around ten such organizations at any one time (see Glasby and Peck, 2004; Miller *et al.*, 2011 for a summary). In many cases, this was due to hostility from *local government*, who saw Care Trusts (which were technically NHS organizations with social care responsibilities and staff delegated to them) as an NHS 'take-over' and as representing loss of local democratic control over local services.

Some Care Trusts were formed in areas with a long history of joint working and were often seen as the logical next step for health and social care communities already working closely together. Many of the early Care Trusts also had stable boundaries between a single local and health authority, as well as local leaders who had been in post for some time and trusted each other. Some Care Trusts were also in relatively small localities who felt they had a unique local identity – and this would not be well served should local health services be drawn into a bigger structure in various NHS reorganizations. They, therefore, sought to protect local services by seeking economies of scale locally, responding in part to fear of external threat. While many areas had this positive history, some did not – and the question for the latter was whether they had enough in common to stay together if the fear of external threat every went away.

Overall, the Care Trusts report some progress in joining up services and offering staff greater career development opportunities. However, the process of organizational merger takes so long and the policy context has shifted so much that it is difficult to identify outcomes for patients and service users that could not have been achieved with a less disruptive form of collaboration (see the entry on *evaluation* for further discussion). Many of the Care Trusts also found it very difficult working in a policy context that did not always seem to recognize their unique, integrated nature – and there were early reports of having to disaggregate activity into 'health' and 'social' care in order to feed up separate performance management systems or of Strategic Health Authorities and inspectors not fully appreciating the differences that being a Care Trust entails. Over time, most Care Trusts have changed form yet again. While provider Care Trusts have sometimes acquired new services as part of the Transforming Community Services agenda, they have also been tasked with becoming FTs (and this legal status trumps the 'Care Trust-ness' given that FT status was not designed with Care Trusts in mind). PCT-based Care Trusts also ceased to exist as their commissioning functions transferred to new CCGs (see, for example, Farnsworth, 2012).

Overall, full merger may not have become as prominent as government initially expected, but Care Trusts represent a major experiment in joint working – and future policy would do well to learn the lessons of this innovation.

Recommendations for policy and practice
- Feedback from Care Trusts suggests that 'they work well where they work' – that is, that they might be a natural next step in some areas but would not necessarily be right elsewhere.
- Joining up front-line services in a system that remains divided can cause frustration and limit potential benefits.
- Staff working in Care Trusts might well argue that *culture* is more important than changing structures – simply being integrated organizationally does not necessarily lead to integrated care.

- Creating new structures is very time consuming, and policy needs to allow sufficient time for new organizations to bed in before they it expects to see improved outcomes.
- Health and social care systems often recognize the need to work together – and with strong commitment, local *leadership* and a supportive policy context fairly radical changes may be possible in local services.

KEY TEXTS

- Glasby, J. and Peck, E. (eds) (2004) *Care Trusts: Partnership Working in Action* (Abingdon: Radcliffe Medical Press)

  Edited collection of contributions looking at the pros and cons of the Care Trust policy, broader issues of organizational culture and local experiences of exploring and implementing Care Trust status.

- Hudson, B. (2002a) 'Ten Reasons Not to Trust Care Trusts', *Managing Community Care*, 10 (2): pp. 3–11

  Early critique of Care Trusts from a leading commentator on health and social care collaboration – see also Hudson (2002b, 2004).

- Miller, R., Dickinson, H. and Glasby, J. (2011) *The Vanguard of Integration or a Lost Tribe? Care Trusts Ten Years On* (Birmingham: Health Services Management Centre)

  Short policy paper reviewing the lessons from Care Trusts, based on interviews with participating Care Trust leaders. Also summarizes the areas which formed Care Trusts and their focus, as well as their likely future in the current policy context.

carers

SEE ALSO **assessment; mixed economy of care**

Although debates about health and social care often focus on formal services and on the role of professional and paid workers, the bulk of support to a range of user groups is provided by family, friends and neighbours on an unpaid basis. While this is often described as *informal care,* this term can sometimes be interpreted in a slightly dismissive manner (as if 'informal' care is less important than formal care – when arguably the opposite is true). This entry therefore uses the term 'carer', albeit that this can sometimes cause confusion and that many 'carers' may not define themselves in this way (but as spouses, children, siblings, friends and so on). Initially, official policy in the United Kingdom did not recognize the needs and contribution of carers – despite the fact that carers make a contribution that has been estimated at £119 billion per year and more than the entire NHS budget (Buckner and Yeandle, 2011). Over time, however, there has been a growing awareness of the vital role that carers play – often driven by the work of carers' campaigning organizations and by research. This has culminated in a range of legal measures and a national strategy to promote the rights of carers and provide greater support (see, for example, HM Government, 2010a). Despite this, the value base of policy makers has not always been clear – are we supporting carers because this is a cheap and effective way of supporting service users? Are we supporting carers because it helps them remain in the labour market (and thus continue paying tax and National Insurance etc.)? Or are we supporting carers because they are citizens too with the same right to a good life as everyone else (see Glasby *et al.*, 2010 for further discussion)?

As a result of these changes, carers now have the right to an assessment of their needs as a carer and to a range of practical and financial supports from the NHS, social care, their employers and the social security system (see Carers UK, 2010 for a summary). However, all the available evidence suggests that carers' experiences – both of being a carer and of health and social care – can be very mixed. While caring *for* somebody implies caring *about* them (and can thus be a very positive and rewarding experience), caring for somebody without adequate support can have negative consequences. Thus, research suggests that caring can have a negative impact on people's health, employment prospects, income and social life, and that carers can sometimes feel either unsupported or taken for granted by the health and social care system (see Glasby, 2012b, ch. 9 for a summary; see also Carers UK, 2004, 2005; Harris *et al.*, 2003; Henwood, 1998; Holzhausen, 2001). Overall, therefore, while there is greater recognition of the role and needs of carers – and greater support available – much remains to be done.

Recommendations for policy and practice
- Carers are the bedrock of the health and social care system – rather than seeing carers as an 'add on' to the support of health

and social care, we should see health and social care as playing a (sometimes very minor) supporting role to the important work that carers do day in and day out.

- Even where services try to support carers, there is a risk that their contribution is taken for granted – the only choice for many people rather than a positive choice for some.
- Although helpful to have a term such as 'carer' to describe an overall group of people with some sort of scope for common experience, many people do not see themselves as 'carers' but as family, friends and neighbours.
- Therefore, there needs to be significant outreach to ensure people are able to access services that have been set up to support them.
- Different policies seem to want to support carers for slightly different reasons – and we may need to be clearer whether we are doing this mainly to support service users, to promote active citizenship or because carers have a right to support.

KEY TEXTS

- Carers UK (2010) *Looking after Someone: A Guide to Carers' Rights and Benefits 2010/11* (London: Carers UK)

  Practical online guide summarizing key rights for carers in terms of money, work and health and social care.

- Clements, L. (2011) *Carers and Their Rights – The Law Relating to Carers.* 4th edn (London: Carers UK)

  Detailed handbook on the law relating to carers produced by a leading carers charity/campaigning group – for further details of the work of Carers UK, see www.carersuk.org.

- HM Government (2010a) *Recognised, Valued and Supported: Next Steps for the Carers Strategy* (London: Department of Health)

Sets out a four-year government strategy to support carers.

child and adolescent mental health

SEE **Children's Trusts**

child protection

SEE **safeguarding**

children and young people

SEE Children's Trusts

Children's Fund

SEE area-based initiatives

Children's Trusts

SEE ALSO Care Trusts; mergers and acquisitions; safeguarding

In English children's services, a key influence has been the Lord Laming review, *Every Child Matters* agenda and the 2004 Children Act introduced in response to the tragic death of Victoria Climbié (Department for Education and Skills, 2003; Laming, 2003). Over time, this has led to the creation of separate children's services, with Councils establishing new children's directorates (made up of education and children's social care) and new adult directorates (with titles such as 'Adults and Communities', 'Health and Social Care' or 'Social Inclusion and Health'). More recently, some Councils have felt that this creates too great a divide between adult and children's services, with some reuniting these directorates (sometimes into new 'people' directorates, incorporating both children's and adult services). In addition, a key part of the broader *Every Child Matter* agenda was a greater emphasis on the *co-location* of staff, information sharing, common *assessment* and improvements in *safeguarding*. While many of these mechanisms were already in place in many adult services, such formal integration was probably less common in some children's services – except in particular pockets (such as teams supporting disabled children or child and adolescent mental health services).

The key vehicle for managing and overseeing these changes was to be the Children's Trust. In practice, there has been significant local variation, with some Children's Trust being real and others more virtual, some focusing on *commissioning* and others on provision and some focusing on particular groups of children and young people. However, there has often been an emphasis on creating more integrated governance structures and on use of pooled funding. In some respects, this mirrors approaches in adult services, via the *Health Act flexibilities* and *Care Trusts*. Indeed, with some adult social care services moving to the NHS and children's services moving increasingly towards *local government*, these emerging arrangements were often seen locally as a form of 'swap'.

In 2009, the tragic case of Peter Connelly (in the same local authority as Victoria Climbié) revealed that these initial reforms had not necessarily had the intended impact, and a further review was conducted by Lord Laming (2009). At the time, there were fears that children's services could see another wholesale reorganization, with all the negative impacts that this can have in the short to medium term (see the entry on *mergers and acquisitions*). Ironically, if this should happen, a policy designed to protect children could arguably put them more at risk as people adjust to new structures and systems.

Recommendations for policy and practice
- Creating increasingly inter-agency children's services and inter-agency adult services runs the risk of creating an even bigger gap between the two at the point of transition. Rather than removing boundaries altogether, perhaps the issue is how we best work across the boundaries we have at any given point in time?
- Like most national initiatives, Children's Trusts seem to have had a different impact in different areas, with issues such as local context and leadership important factors.
- Like any major merger or structural change, there is a risk that the subsequent upheaval could increase risks in the short term.
- It takes time and commitment to build new relationships and trust, so new structures need enough stability to be able to get up and running and start to deliver.
- Front-line practitioners need time and support to begin to work in new way, and the key challenges may well be *cultural* rather than structural.

KEY TEXTS
- Bachman, M. *et al.* (2009) 'Integrating Children's Services in England: National Evaluation of Children's Trusts', *Child: Care, Health and Development*, 35 (2): pp. 257–265
  Article summarizing key findings from the national evaluation of Children's Trusts.

- Kellett, M. (2011) *Children's Perspectives on Integrated Services* (Basingstoke: Palgrave Macmillan)

  Leading textbook reviewing the Every Child Matters agenda and focusing in particular on children's views of integrated care.

- Laming, H. (2003) *The Victoria Climbié Inquiry* (London: HMSO)
- Laming, H. (2009) *The Protection of Children in England: A Progress Report* (London: TSO)

  Two national reviews of children's services in the wake of high profile and very tragic child deaths.

choice and competition

SEE **markets**

chronic disease

SEE **long-term conditions**

Clinical Commissioning Groups

SEE ALSO **commissioning; Health and Well-Being Board; joint commissioning; NHS Commissioning Boards; primary care**

As explained in the *commissioning* entry, CCGs are the latest in a long line of primary care-led forms of health care commissioning. Introduced by the Health and Social Care Act of 2012, they will take responsibility for commissioning the vast majority of local *community* and *acute* health care (responsible for around £60 billion of the NHS budget). They will be authorized by a new *NHS Commissioning Board* (which will be accountable to the Secretary of State for the overall outcomes achieved by the NHS) and will be able to choose where they get their commissioning support from (although the NHS is developing a series of local Commissioning Support Services who will offer their services to the new CCGs). In difficult financial circumstances, these reforms aim at placing *primary care* clinicians (especially general practitioners or GPs) centre stage and to give general practice greater control of the system and a greater financial incentive to use scarce resources as effectively as possible. However, there has been significant professional and media debate as to whether this will change the nature of GPs' relationships with their patients, whether GPs will want to be commissioners, what support they will need and how much the new system may cost. A more detailed history of NHS commissioning is provided in the commissioning entry.

Recommendations for policy and practice

- Greater clinical engagement in commissioning seems a crucial goal with widespread support. However, the system that is emerging in England seems to have a number of similarities with previous models of primary care-led commissioning – perhaps similar results could have been achieved without so much structural and legislative change?
- Front-line staff may often have focused on joint working between community health and *social care* services – but GPs are likely to be significant new players in an era of clinical commissioning.
- The NHS is being asked to save large amounts of money and implement major organizational changes all at the same time – and this level of upheaval all at once is unprecedented.
- A series of key questions remain unanswered around the relationship between CCGs, *Health and Well-Being Boards*, Commissioning Support Services and the *NHS Commissioning Board*.
- GPs will now be providers of some services as well as commissioners for the bulk of local health services for local populations – it is not yet fully clear how potential conflicts of interest are to be avoided.

KEY TEXTS

- The Coalition's initial vision for the NHS is setting out in its 2010 White Paper, *Liberating the NHS* (Department of Health, 2010a)
- Timmins, N. (2012) *Never Again? The Story of the Health and Social Care Act 2012* (London: King's Fund)

  Written by a former national journalist, this is a fascinating account of the Coalition government and the events that shaped the Health and Social Act. This is a rapidly emerging area of policy and practice, but the key texts in the commissioning entry provide helpful background and context.

clinical networks

SEE ALSO clinical pathways; networks

Over the last decade or so, there has been sustained interest in the notion of clinical networks from UK governments and local health care organizations alike. This interest also reflects wider international attention that has been paid to these forms (see, for example, Braithwaite *et al.*, 2009). In the UK, clinical networks have largely focused on creating links between health care organizations. Typically this has been as a way of linking secondary and tertiary care organizations with primary health care organizations. In integration terms then, clinical networks have primarily been used as a way of attempting to create vertical links (i.e. between health organizations) rather than horizontal links (i.e. between health and other sectors).

The need for these types of arrangements has arisen out of what Ferlie *et al.* (2010) refer to as the post-Fordist era of health care. Many hospitals in the UK and other parts of the world have increasingly become specialized and as such have often lost multidisciplinary and community-based health services. This fragmentation has been compounded by the use of a range of different types of public, private and third sector providers and so clinical networks have been seen as a way of maintaining sustainable and comprehensive access to care (6 *et al.*, 2006). Today we have access to a number of information sharing technologies that should also help us to facilitate these networks in a way that has not been possible in the past.

Clinical networks (or managed clinical networks or managed networks as they are sometimes known) tend to exist around particular diseases (e.g. cancer and diabetes), particular specialty groups (e.g. specialist paediatric services and neurology) or client groups (e.g. older people and children).

The Calman-Hine report (1995) was influential in suggesting that cancer services needed to be delivered through networks of professionals, rather than buildings. Ultimately this report suggested that clinical networks should be able to reduce delays in diagnosis and treatment by bringing professionals together in such a way. Clinical networks are advocated on the basis that they should (NHS Confederation, 2002)

- make more efficient use of staff;
- reduce professional and organizational boundaries;
- share good practice;
- put the patient at the centre of care; and
- improve access to care.

Yet Goodwin *et al.* (2004, p. 310) conclude that faith in clinical networks is often based on 'a series of hypothetical advantages' like those set out by the NHS Confederation, rather than 'known outcomes'. Indeed, there remains little equivocal evidence that points to networks being generally a good thing and most evidence suggests that these need significant investment to make them work. Ferlie *et al.* (2010) found that at their best clinical networks developed front-line processes that allowed sharing and learning across organizational boundaries. However, they also found that there were a number of disadvantages such as networks turning into a series of meetings and little output; lack of focus; need for administrative resourcing to keep energy up; problems in performance management; high transaction costs; tendency to get dominated by national targets (rather than local); and a potential lack of innovation capacity.

Recommendations for policy and practice
- The increasing specialization of health care and the use of information technologies means that some co-ordinating mechanism is necessary to make patient experience streamlined through the range of health care providers that they may come into contact with during the period of care.
- There are many different possible types of network arrangements, so stakeholders need to be clear about what they are trying to do and what impact they hope this will have on a range of organizational, professional and service user outcomes.
- There is little evidence to demonstrate that clinical networks are innately a 'good thing'. Implementation of clinical networks by itself does not guarantee that positive outcomes will be delivered.
- There may be negative implications of introducing networks and not all potential impacts are positive.
- Staff working in front-line practice may need to think about their work in different ways in the future, and the concept of clinical networks may prove helpful in developing new perspectives and approaches.

KEY TEXTS

- 6, P. et al. (2006) *Managing Networks of Twenty-First Century Organisations* (Basingstoke: Palgrave Macmillan)

  This book provides a review of the literature pertaining to networks across a range of different sectors and applies this knowledge to a health and social care context.

- Ferlie, E. *et al.* (2010) *Networks in Health Care: A Comparative Study of Their Management, Impact and Performance.* Report for the National Institute for Health Research Service Delivery and Organisation Programme, SDO Project (08/1518/102) (London: Department of Management, Kings College London)

  This report sets out research conducted into clinical networks in the NHS and assesses the degree to which they have been successful.

- Nolte, E., Knai, C. and McKee, M. (2008) *Managing Chronic Conditions: Experience in Eight Countries*, Observatory Studies Series No. 15 (Copenhagen: World Health Organization, European Observatory on Health Systems and Policies)

  This text includes some commentary on different national experiences of dealing with chronic care.

clinical pathways

SEE ALSO **clinical networks**

As the fields of health and social care have become increasingly specialized in terms of the focus of individual agencies and professionals and as the range of agencies and organizations has expanded, the journeys of care that patients experience have often become more complex. Clinical pathways have become a way to manage quality and experience of care and also a way in which care processes can be standardized. Bryan *et al.* (2002, pp. 77–78) describe an integrated care pathway as 'a map of the process involved in managing a common clinical condition or situation. It should detail what to do, when to do it, by whom the action should be undertaken and where the task should be performed.' A key component of clinical pathways is also their evidence-based nature, with *The NHS Plan* (Department of Health, 2000) emphasizing the importance of planning care around the patient and the use of protocols for each condition to ensure evidence-based practice.

Beyond the sorts of broad aims that are set out above, there is more debate concerning what this concept is precisely. Kinsman *et al.* (2010) identify 84 different terms that may mean clinical pathway, including care map, integrated care pathway, protocol, guideline and critical care pathway. From an extensive review of the literature, they argue that five criteria can be used to define a clinical pathway. The first of these must be present to be defined as a clinical pathway, along with three of the other four criteria. These criteria are as follows:

- The intervention is a structured multidisciplinary plan of care.
- The intervention is used to translate guidelines or evidence into local structures.
- The intervention details the steps in a course or treatment or care in a plan, pathway, algorithm, guideline, protocol or other 'inventory of actions'.
- The intervention has timeframes or criteria-based progression.
- The intervention aims at standardizing care for a specific clinical problem, procedure or episode of healthcare in a specific population.

As these criteria demonstrate, an important component of clinical pathways is that they involve a local interpretation of evidence-based guidelines and that this is done via a multidisciplinary team so that we can gain input from a range of different professionals. By virtue of a range of different professionals coming together, it is thought that this can promote better joint working. However, with this in mind, it is crucial that joint working processes are promoted and, for example, one professional group does not dominate over others. The benefits of closer joint working will not emerge simply by virtue of instigating a clinical pathway. Hindle and Yazbeck (2005) report that one way to help this process is to improve the understanding that health professionals have of clinical pathways.

Clinical pathways have been associated with a range of benefits such as more efficient use of resources, higher quality of care and better teamwork. However, a number of authors have warned against assuming that positive outcomes will automatically flow from working on clinical pathways. There are a range of other impacts such as the redrawing of professional boundaries and the deskilling of professionals through the introduction of standardized pathways. There are also a range of barriers to the introduction of clinical pathways that need to be considered such as a lack of resource to support the development of clinical pathways and lack of acceptance of multidisciplinary practice by some medical practitioners. Anticipating these issues in advance can greatly improve the degree of success that clinical pathways have.

Recommendations for policy and practice

- There are many different definitions of clinical pathways, so it is important that different partners are clear precisely what it is that is being referred to when using this term.
- Clinical pathways can be a helpful way to encourage interdisciplinary working, provided that the processes to facilitate this are established in a way that promotes joint working.
- Clinical pathways can have a number of positive impacts, but they may also have some negative implications and it is important that these are taken into consideration.
- The literature suggests some of the types of barriers that might hinder the development of clinical pathways and these needs to be carefully considered.
- For front-line practitioners, the concept of clinical pathways can help us to think about the patient's journey in a more holistic way.

KEY TEXTS

- Atwal, A. and Caldwell, K. (2002) 'Do Multidisciplinary Integrated Care Pathways Improve Interprofessional Collaboration?' *Scandinavian Journal Caring Sciences*, 16: pp. 360–367

  This paper reviews the evidence about the impacts of care pathways on interprofessional collaboration.

- Bragato, L. and Jacobs, K. (2003) 'Care Pathways: The Road to Better Health Services?' *Journal of Health Organization and Management*, 17 (3): pp. 164–180

  This paper considers whether care pathways improve the delivery of quality in health services.

- Kinsman, L. *et al.* (2010) 'What Is a Clinical Pathway? Development of a Definition to Inform the Debate', *BMC Medicine*, 8: p. 31

  This literature review provides a helpful introduction to the definition of clinical pathways.

collaboration

SEE partnership working

commissioning

SEE ALSO **Clinical Commissioning Groups; markets; mixed economy of care; New Public Management**

Under the 'internal market' of the 1990s, the NHS adopted a series of more *market*-based reforms. Henceforth, one set of agencies was to be responsible for deciding what services an area needed, finding a provider and paying for these services, while other agencies were responsible for providing health care. The organizations responsible for securing services on behalf of the local population (later described as 'commissioning') have included a range of agencies over time: in England, the key agencies were health authorities, GP fundholders, Primary Care Groups, PCTs and CCGs.

Initially, PCTs were responsible both for buying primary and hospital services for local people as well as providing a range of *community health services* (such as district nursing, health visiting, etc.). From the mid-2000s, however, PCTs were increasingly recast as commissioning-led organizations, and were asked to divest themselves of their provision altogether (with PCT provider services often integrating with *acute care*, forming a *social enterprise*, integrating with *local government* or establishing a Community FT). To support this change in emphasis, the New Labour governments (1997–2010) developed a national 'world class commissioning' agenda, with each PCT undergoing an annual assurance process in order to demonstrate its progress against a series of organizational competences (Department of Health, 2007a).

Following the 2010 general election, the Conservative/Liberal Democrat Coalition government introduced legal and policy changes to abolish PCTs and Strategic Health Authorities, replacing them with new local CCGs, an *NHS Commissioning Board* and a series of local Commissioning Support Services (Department of Health, 2010a). In many ways, this returned to elements of the pre-1997 system, where previous Conservative governments had experimented with different forms of GP-led commissioning (known as 'GP fundholding' and 'total purchasing pilots' or 'TPPs'). Reviews of these previous measures suggested some benefits in terms of access to care and the development of new services in the community, but also raised concerns that such measures might increase costs and/or create a two-tier system (where people with a fundholding GP could get better services than those without – see, for example, Le Grand *et al.*, 1998; Mannion, 2011). The broader literature also suggests that major *structural change* often only ever partially achieves stated objectives, typically failing to save the money anticipated, reducing morale and productivity and stalling positive service development for up to two years or so after the initial change (for an accessible summary, see Edwards, 2010). Despite this, NHS commissioning structures have been repeatedly reformed over time – arguably weakening them in relation to service providers (who have remained relatively stable).

In social care, the NHS and Community Care Act 1990 turned social workers into care managers, responsible for *assessing* individual needs and designing subsequent care packages from a more *mixed economy* of care. *Local government* was also expected to more fully separate its purchasing and its provision, and in-house services were increasingly challenged to be fully competitive compared to alternative service providers in the *private* or *voluntary* sectors. This has since resulted in the situation where the bulk of the care home market in particular is dominated by private provision, with some voluntary provision and a small number of *public* providers. More recently, adult social care has recast individual *service users* as micro-commissioners of their own care with the advent of the *personalization* agenda.

Recommendations for policy and practice
- Many previous reforms have seemed to assume that there is a perfect organizational structure out there – but that we just have not found it yet (and if we keep going, the perfect structure might be just one more reorganization away).
- In contrast, the evidence (both research and past experience) suggests that major structural changes only ever partially achieve stated objectives and can have a series of unintended negative consequences. A major irony of successive NHS reorganizations of the commissioning function is that they may have weakened commissioning relative to the stability of health care providers (albeit while trying to strengthen commissioning).

- Constant change can make joint working between the NHS and local government even harder, as it disrupts existing relationships and ways of working.
- Greater clinical engagement in commissioning seems a crucial goal – but the abolition of previous structures and the wholesale transfer of power to new CCGs seems a risky way of trying to achieve this. There are also unanswered questions as to how the NHS changes will fit with the development of the personalization agenda in social care.
- Real issues remain about the extent to which GPs want to be commissioners, feel comfortable with their new role or have the skills to do this well.

KEY TEXTS

- Glasby, J. (2012a) *Commissioning for Health and Well-Being: An Introduction* (Bristol: The Policy Press)

  Offers an introduction to commissioning in health and social care, exploring different stages of the commissioning cycle and a broader range of cross-cutting themes such as the economics of commissioning, user involvement in commissioning, joint commissioning and commissioning in an era of personalization.

- Mays, N., Dixon, A. and Jones, L. (2011) *Understanding New Labour's Market Reforms of the English NHS* (London: King's Fund)

  Edited collection exploring the impact of market mechanisms on the NHS.

- Smith, J. et al. (2004) *A Review of the Effectiveness of Primary-Care Led Commissioning and Its Place in the UK NHS* (London: Health Foundation)

  Key review of experience of primary care-led commissioning in the different countries of the United Kingdom and of the evidence base to date.

community services

SEE ALSO **acute care; Clinical Commissioning Groups; commissioning; mixed economy of care; primary care; social care; social enterprise**

Health care has historically been organized on the basis of *primary care*/general practice, community services and *acute care* – with the middle of these arguably neglected at the expense of the others. Acute hospitals are often very popular and powerful institutions, while GPs have a key role as a gateway into the rest of the system and are often very trusted by the public. In contrast, community health services (such as district nursing, health visitors, etc.) – although crucial – can sometimes seem like something of an afterthought in policy terms. Although social care organizes itself in different ways, there are clear opportunities for community health and social care services to work together in a number of different ways – whether through multi-professional *teamworking, co-location* and/or more formal integration (perhaps via new integrated *social enterprises* or Community FTs).

In England, the *Transforming Community Services* agenda led to former PCTs divesting themselves of their provider services so as to focus solely on being a 'world class commissioner'. While some services were big enough to become standalone Community FTs or social enterprises, others merged into larger acute or mental health trusts (often described as a form of 'vertical integration' between hospital and the community – as opposed to 'horizontal integration' between community-based services). Although this may offer the chance to deliver more integrated care and to shift some hospital-based services closer to home, the risk is that community services are sucked into a model dominated by acute pressures and that it becomes even harder to develop community alternatives. The use of Foundation status also means that some areas will have newly emerging CCGs keen to flex their muscles, coupled with relatively autonomous and standalone community and acute Trusts – making joint working even harder. For social care colleagues, there is a dilemma about where to focus collaborative energy – with provision or with *commissioning*? There is also a risk that the timescales accompanying Transforming Community Services might have led in some areas to a single organizational 'solution' (essentially a single place to put community services en masse), rather than a more nuanced attempt to explore which services would flourish best in which settings and with which partners.

Recommendations for policy and practice
• Community services are crucial in an era of *long-term conditions* and to develop care closer to home – yet have often seemed neglected by policy at the expense of other parts of the system.

- Integrating acute and community services could not only improve links between hospital and the community, but could also suck care out of the community into hospitals (which is arguably the wrong way round).
- In England, *Transforming Community Services* could have been an opportunity to develop more integrated approaches, with different services moving in different directions. In practice, tight timescales may have prompted some areas to opt for a single organizational structure and place services en masse (which could create future barriers to joint working).
- For front-line staff there is a real risk of feeling change weary as yet another structural change takes place without necessarily helping people to understand current priorities and how their practice may need to develop in new ways in the future.

KEY TEXTS

- This seems an under-researched area, but a key contribution has been made by Helen Parker (2006, 2009), who has reviewed the evidence on behalf of the NHS Institute and the Department of Health. (See also Parker and Glasby, 2008a, 2008b for articles on the reform of community services and on key barriers in local practice.)
- The Department of Health (2010b, 2011a) has published a series of online guides to transforming community services (see www.dh.gov. uk /en/Publicationsandstatistics/Publications/PublicationsPolicyAnd Guidance/DH_124178) and slides that provide an overview of the programme (available via http://www.dh.gov.uk/en/Healthcare/TCS / index.htm).
- Singh, D. (2006) *Making the Shift: Key Success Factors – A Rapid Review of Best Practice in Shifting Hospital Care into the Community* (Birmingham: Health Services Management Centre/NHS Institute) Rapid review of the evidence behind attempts to shift care from hospital into the community.

confidentiality

SEE **data protection**

co-location

SEE ALSO **culture; teamwork**

Co-location is often cited as one of the factors that can help support effective inter-agency working and has been a widely used approach in primary and community care. At its most basic, co-location involves teams being located in the same physical space. For example, Brown *et al.* (2003) describe the creation of an integrated health and social care team serving older people and their carers. In order to encourage greater collaboration, community-based offices were located in GP practices and sought to bring together social workers, social work assistants, occupational therapists, occupational therapy assistants and district nurses.

Co-location is often advocated on the basis that it should afford team members more opportunity to come into contact with one another on both a formal and informal basis.

In terms of the formal, being located together may allow teams to develop joint paperwork or allow them to refer service users to their colleagues more quickly than if based in different locations. In terms of the less formal, being located in the same building might afford professionals a better understanding of their colleagues and their roles, responsibilities and organizational pressures. Over time the building up of this familiarity might, for example, lead professionals to create joint processes or trust their partners to conduct particular aspects of *assessment* processes. Co-location is also highlighted as being a helpful contributor in creating an integrated *culture*.

Although co-location may hold the potential to deliver a number of benefits, we should not simply assume that if we co-locate teams that this will produce more effective inter-professional working. While a number of claims are made for co-location, the research evidence does not show that co-location always lead to substantially closer inter-professional working (Davey *et al.*, 2005) or to improved outcomes for service users (Brown *et al.*, 2003). Although co-location may alter how much direct communication professionals have with one another, it does not necessarily alter the quality or effectiveness of communication. This means that attempts to foster closer inter-agency working relationships through co-location need to be accompanied by development activities; simply basing professionals in the same physical space is not enough.

In some cases, co-location might even be seen as threatening. Kharicha *et al.* (2005) report that co-location may pose threats for social workers. In this study, social workers did not feel that co-location encouraged health colleagues to understand their role. Furthermore, rather than encouraging a more informal process of referrals, social workers often wanted an increase in formality of referrals, so they go through the appropriate channels and not, for example, a note left on a desk late in the day. In this study, social workers also talked about the potential to feel isolated from their profession that might also occur from co-location. This isolation could lead to difficulties for social workers in working to social care priorities as there may be conflicts that arise from competing agendas.

Recommendations for policy and practice
- Co-location can be a helpful tool in bringing teams together and encouraging more effective inter-agency working.
- Front-line staffs often say that they do not have enough contact with or knowledge of people from different professional backgrounds, and that they would like opportunity to meet each other and get to know each other better.
- Often, they stress the importance of informal contact – being able to discuss a referral or seek advice over the coffee machine or the photocopier.
- However, simply locating teams in the same building might not necessarily bring about improvements in services by itself. Co-located teams need investment so that they can be encouraged to interact with one another and to build up formal and informal relationships.
- Without being carefully managed, co-location may even potentially have an adverse impact on some professionals, so the implications of this need to be carefully considered.

KEY TEXTS
- Brown, L., Tucker, C. and Domokos, T. (2003) 'Evaluating the Impact of Integrated Health and Social Care Teams on Older People Living in the Community', *Health and Social Care in the Community*, 11: pp. 85–94
  This paper provides a worked example of where teams set out to co-locate and the outcomes of this process of integration.

- Kharicha, K. et al. (2005) 'Tearing Down the Berlin Wall: Social Workers' Perspectives on Joint Working with General Practice', *Family Practice*, 22: pp. 399–405
  This paper provides an account of co-location from the perspective of social workers.

co-production

SEE ALSO involvement; personalization; power

In the context of a text about inter-agency working, the notion of co-production illuminates a different form of collaboration. This mode of collaboration focuses on the relationship between service users and public services – and not the more horizontal linkages between different public sector agencies. The concept of co-production has a significant history that originally arose from the civil rights movement from the United States (New Economics Foundation, 2008).

Cummins and Miller (2007, p. 8) define co-production as about how 'services have to learn how to *work with* rather than *do unto* service users.' In this vein it is argued that co-production is necessary because of the limitations of traditional modes of delivering public services where professionals are 'experts' and their relationship can often be paternalistic with the professional holding the power. Over the years, we have increasingly heard calls from a number of different individuals and organizations suggesting that these sorts of relationships are neither effective nor efficient. Co-production has been seen as a way of overcoming some of these limitations and putting service users and patients more firmly centre-stage in the design, delivery and audit of public services. As such it is about a fundamental change to the ethos of service delivery.

As suggested above, there is not one simple influence that can be identified that has led to the interest in co-production. Instead we can identify a series of different pressures that have called for reform, including the following:

- Existing models of health and social care delivery are argued by some to give poor value for money. Co-production has been seen as a way of increasing efficiency and reducing public spending (Boyle, 2004).
- Service users are more likely to hold expertise about the particular nature of their life and any challenges that they face. With changes to technology and the increasingly use of new media, moreover, professionals may no longer have more information than service users (Coulter and Ellins, 2006).

- The concept of *personalization* has gained prominence, and this argues that services should be controlled and shaped by those who use them, rather than by public bodies alone (Glasby and Littlechild, 2009).
- Both health and social care organizations have attempted to devolve power downwards, to a local level and also towards frontline staff (Needham and Carr, 2009). They have also developed greater commitment over time to notions of involving and engaging patients and service users – both in decisions about individual care and in the organization of services more generally.
- Public sector organizations have shown a growing interest in creating social capital within local communities (Cummins and Miller, 2007).

Given that it has a number of potential drivers, co-production may vary in a number of different ways when translated into practice: involving different types of collaborative relationships; involving different numbers of individuals; taking place at different stages; involving different types of skills and taking place at different levels. For a more detailed overview of these different factors, see Needham and Carr (2009) in relation to social care and Realpe and Wallace (2010) in relation to health.

Although attempts at co-production might look very different in practice, what unites them is a sense that this can be transformative, leading to very different types of services and outcomes for service users (Needham and Carr, 2009). This is particularly the case in relation to those individuals who have long-term health conditions and require the input of both health and social care professionals. Co-production can actively support self-management (Realpe and Wallace, 2010) and in turn deliver better quality and more relevant and cheaper services in a way that actively engages patients and service users in their own care.

Recommendations for policy and practice
- Co-production means putting service users at the heart of the design, delivery and audit of health and social care services and therefore offers the potential for fundamental reform of the way that public services are delivered.

- There are a range of different pressures that have led to co-production being seen as a important mechanism and it may be helpful to be clear about which of these drivers you are attempting to address when attempting co-production initiatives.
- In principle, there may be scope to create an approach that feels exciting and liberating for staff and for service users.
- In practice, co-production may look or feel very different according to what it is trying to achieve. There is no one right way to organize co-production.
- There is evidence that co-production can lead to improvements in terms of service user outcomes and the efficiency of services.

KEY TEXTS
- Boyle, D. *et al.* (2010) *Right Here, Right Now: Taking Co-Production into the Mainstream* (London: NESTA)

  This report is one of a series into the issue of co-production published by NESTA that provide helpful introductions to the concept of co-production.

- Needham, C. and Carr, S. (2009) *Co-Production: An Emerging Evidence Base for Adult Social Care Transformation* (London: Social Care Institute for Excellence)

  This report reviews the concept of co-production and the evidence for this in the context of adult social care.

- Realpe, A. and Wallace, L.M. (2010) *What Is Co-Production?* (London: The Health Foundation)

  This report provides an overview of the concept of co-production and its application in the context of health care.

culture

SEE ALSO co-location; teamwork; values

In discussions of inter-agency working, one topic seems to recur more than any other: culture. In reading accounts of inter-agency work, we often hear that some initiative was not successful because the partners coming together had very different cultures, or conversely that joint working was successful because the cultures were very similar. Indeed, the wider commercial sector literature on *mergers and acquisitions* suggests that these most often fail because structural factors take precedence over the more human (cultural) factors. However, despite the frequency of its occurrence, this concept has often been treated in a rather simplistic manner as a factor that should be attended to, but without being any clearer about what that factor might actually look like in practice. This can be problematic as culture is a rather complex concept with many different underpinning models suggested by various commentators.

Looking at the literature, there are three main models of culture as identified by Meyerson and Martin (1987). Most often when people talk about culture they are assuming an 'integration model' of culture. This means that culture is a factor that organizations possess, that it is fairly consistent across organizations and that we can easily recognize this culture. In simple terms, we can define this model of culture as 'the way we do things around here' (Ouchi and Johnson, 1978). Working to this kind of model of culture suggests that we can intervene to change culture and that if we are trying to enhance inter-agency working then what we need to do is make the cultures of the partner agencies more alike.

A second model of culture is called the 'difference model' and this suggests that culture is more differentiated and pluralistic. Rather than there being one recognisable culture within an organization there may be a several, with different interest groups having slightly different cultures. So if the first model recognizes health and social care organizations as having different health and social cultures, the second would further breakdown a health culture into medical, nursing and management cultures, etc. Like the first model, culture is still considered a factor that can be changed so that groups might work together more effectively.

The final approach to culture is the 'ambiguity model'. This describes culture as being more personal and local than the other two models, and this is something that is constantly being negotiated and re-negotiated between individuals and groups within an organization. The organization might have some impact on this process of negotiation – but it is the least predictable and open to manipulation of the three models. Culture is not formed by the organization or the professional group, but by the interaction of individuals.

In health and social care, we most often see the use of the integration model in explaining the difficulty in working across health and social care boundaries. The NHS is typically characterized as a universal service, which is procedurally regimented and top-down in style, concerned with the treatment of conditions according to national targets. Social services, on the other hand, focus on the most vulnerable, with a practical focus but sometimes challenged in terms of strategy and are concerned with the holistic care of individuals according to local needs and with local discretion (see Wistow and Waddington, 2006 for further detail on this). Some of the differences between health and social care are not only due to the ways in which services are structured, but these are also linked to more human factors. This is an important point, as it suggests that just changing structures will not change cultures. In fact there is evidence to illustrate that when structural change happens it makes professionals *more* attached to their professional culture, which makes inter-agency working more challenging (Peck *et al.*, 2002).

So is the management of culture possible? The literature suggests that 'cultural management in the sense of creating an enduring set of shared beliefs is impossible' (Parker, 2000, p. 28) – which may dismay some given that culture plays an important factor in the success of inter-agency working. However, there is agreement that some changes to culture can be effected, but that large-scale culture shifts rarely happen. Is culture change desirable? There is little empirical evidence linking culture change and organizational performance, but it intuitively seems likely that there is some form of link. However, there is also a warning. Much of the synergy that comes from inter-agency working is the outcome of different cultures working together. If cultures are broken down and are *too* similar, some of the value of joint working might be lost.

Recommendations for policy and practice
- When undertaking any form of change process, ignore human factors such as culture at your peril. Ultimately these will likely make the largest contribution to the relative success of any significant change, and failing to attend to these factors could lead to failure.
- Be clear what you mean when you talk about culture – you might not necessarily share the same assumptions as your colleagues or partners about what this term means and therefore how (or indeed if) you might be able to intervene in this factor.

- Structural change alone will not create cultural change and in the short-term may actually make people more attached to existing professional cultures.
- Organizational culture change may be achieved partially through redesign, but there will be unanticipated consequences.
- Do not assume that breaking down differences in cultures is always a positive thing.

KEY TEXTS

- Bate, P. (1995) *Strategies for Cultural Change* (Oxford: Butterworth-Heinemann)

  This provides a good account of ways in which to approach cultural change in health care.

- Meyerson, D. and Martin, J. (1987) 'Cultural Change: An Integration of Three Different Views', *Journal of Management Studies*, 24: pp. 623–643

  This provides a good overview of different models of culture.

- Peck, E. and Dickinson, H. (2009) 'Partnership Working and Organisational Culture' in J. Glasby and H. Dickinson (eds) *International Perspectives on Health and Social Care: Partnership Working in Action* (Oxford: Wiley-Blackwell)

  This reviews the international literature on inter-agency working and culture – other chapters in this edited collection also touch on linked topics.

d

data protection

SEE ALSO **culture; values**

There are many examples where the failure to share information between professionals has been a contributory factor in the failure of public services. The Bichard inquiry into the Soham murders cited the failure of Humberside police to pass on information about Ian Huntley as a key failing. Similarly, the Laming report into the death of Victoria Climbié highlighted the failure to collect information and share concerns across multiple agency boundaries. In both these cases, a failure to share data was a key focus of the subsequent inquiries.

Yet in practice, professionals often cite difficulties both with the processes in place to help share data and the principles that underpin what data can be shared and with whom. Indeed, one of the reasons given for why information on Ian Huntley was not shared and which the Bichard inquiry spent some time investigating related to confusion over the principles of the Data Protection Act 1998. While this Act is concerned with the ways that personal data is held, stored and shared, there are other influential forces at play such as those of the NHS Confidentiality Code (which incorporates the principles of the Caldicott Report) and human rights legislation. As Dow explains, 'the law on data sharing is complex and uncertain. On the one hand, the Caldicott principles are emphasizing the importance of patient and service user confidentiality; on the other hand, the priority given to child protection and, increasingly, adult protection emphasizes the importance of over-riding confidentiality where there is a risk of significant harm to the child or adult' (2005, p. 11).

Key legal frameworks and requirements include the Data Protection Act 1998, Article 8 of the Human Rights Act 1998 (which focuses on respect for private and family life) and the Freedom of Information Act 2000. Local areas will also have a 'Caldicott

Guardian' (introduced initially in the NHS and later extended to social care) – to safeguard and govern use of personal data.

These are complex issues, but helpful summaries are often available in official guidance and in legal textbooks (see, for example, Department of Health, 2003a; Mandelstam, 2008). However, such legal and technical requirements are only part of the story. Just as important (perhaps even more important) are the different professional attitudes to and practices around information sharing/withholding at practice level (which are more *cultural* in nature). Whatever national legislation and guidance say, this is interpreted (often imperfectly) at local level and contributes over time to different approaches to patient/client confidentiality. Arguably these cultural differences are harder to tackle than some of the legal issues (where clear guidance and communication could help to improve the situation). When different professional cultures are at stake, the issues are often much more difficult to identify, diagnose and resolve – as they relate to deeply held personal and professional views about what constitutes good practice and about 'how we do things round here' (see the entry on *culture* for further discussion).

Overall, different professional cultures combine with a series of legal and policy pressures, and this can cause significant conflict and tension for local agencies and workers seeking to strike a balance between ensuring confidentiality, protecting people's data and sharing information with different professions. While there are no easy answers, Richardson and Asthana (2005a) suggest that it is important 'to acknowledge such tensions, and to accept that they are regularly managed by front-line staff in their attempts to do their best for service users in the wider society' (p. 5). These authors go on to provide a framework of information sharing that sets out four possible scenarios:

1. Where information is withheld inappropriately and without good cause and information is shared inappropriately or without good cause, there is high risk of breaching confidentiality and high risk of neglecting to pass on important information.
2. Where information is withheld inappropriately and without good cause and information is shared with good cause and

appropriately, there is low risk of breaching confidentiality
and high risk of neglecting to pass on important information.

3. Where information is withheld with good cause and
   appropriately and information is shared inappropriately
   or without good cause, there is high risk of breaching
   confidentiality and low risk of neglecting to pass on important
   information.

4. Where information is withheld with good cause and
   appropriately and information is shared with cause and
   appropriately, there is low risk of breaching confidentiality
   and low risk of neglecting to pass on important information.
   (Richardson and Asthana, 2005a, p. 50)

Richardson and Asthana suggest that this can be helpful for organizations in order to map their various practices and think about
where they might like them to be. As this framework shows, pattern
B might be seen as over-cautious, whereas C is possibly overly open.
While pattern A is rather chaotic, D might be seen as an ideal mode
of information sharing.

Often one of the issues that is focused on in debates about information sharing and data protection is that of technical aspects
and the compatibility (or more often incompatibility) of different
data systems. However, as we have suggested above, this is not a
panacea in terms of producing effective information sharing (Keen
and Denby, 2009). How professionals are trained and supported to
be able to understand and navigate the tensions of data protection
and confidentiality is crucial. For example, different professional
and organizational *cultures* have quite different perspectives in
terms of what information it is acceptable to share and what should
remain confidential (Richardson and Asthana, 2005b). Therefore,
individuals and organizations need to pay attention to these 'softer'
issues as well as the more technical aspects of data protection and
information sharing.

Recommendations for policy and practice
- The issue of data protection and information sharing is a key
  component of providing safe and high-quality public services.
- Local health and social care organizations have a series
  of legal and policy duties in relation to the storage and sharing

of information and these can cause tensions in practice.
- Professionals may find it helpful to think through their behaviours in relation to information sharing and the impacts that this has in terms of confidentiality across a range of different practices.
- The extent to which information systems are compatible with one another play an important role in sharing information.
- Data protection is more than simply a technical issue and requires investment in training, staff support and culture change.

KEY TEXTS
- Department of Health (2003a) *Confidentiality: NHS Code of Practice* (London: Department of Health)

  This document provides guidance to the NHS and NHS-related organizations on patient information confidentiality issues.

- Keen, J. and Denby, T. (2009) 'Partnerships in the Digital Age' in J. Glasby and H. Dickinson (eds), *International Perspectives on Health and Social Care: Partnership Working in Action* (Oxford: Wiley-Blackwell)

  This book chapter provides an overview of the issues relating to networked electronic services in the context of inter-agency working.

- Richardson, S. and Asthana, S. (2005a) 'Policy and Legal Influences on Inter-Organisational Information Sharing in Health and Social Care Services', *Journal of Integrated Care*, 13 (3): pp. 3–10

  This article provides a helpful overview of the policy and legal structures that impact on inter-organizational information sharing.

delayed discharge/transfers of care

SEE **hospital discharge**

devolution

SEE ALSO **Health Boards (Wales and Scotland); Health and Social Care Trusts (Northern Ireland); Joint Future (Scotland)**

At its most simple, devolution essentially means the granting of powers from a national level to a regional or local level. In terms of UK health and social care, there are at least two ways in which devolution has occurred. The first is in terms of the political devolution from Whitehall to Scotland, Northern Ireland and Wales. The second is in terms of the devolution of power within individual institutions and the sorts of responsibilities and *accountabilities* that NHS and social care organizations have in practice. This section mainly focuses on the first on these issues, although before moving on to this we reflect briefly on the latter point.

In inter-agency working, one of the issues that can cause difficulty is the different responsibilities and powers that individuals and agencies hold. Broadly speaking, the NHS has tended to be a more centralized decision-making system, while *local government* has more devolved decision-making powers over their services. This is a broad generalization, but the key point here is that the different decision-making processes of these institutions can pose challenges when working together. Both the NHS and Local Authorities have undergone a number of changes in recent years in an attempt to balance the competing aims of local discretion over services and attempting to avoid a form of 'postcode lottery' where very different services are offered across areas.

In terms of political devolution, the various constituent countries of the United Kingdom have argued over time that the sorts of challenges that they face are unique (or at least different in a number of significant ways). Indeed, public health figures show a significant difference in terms of the prevalence of obesity, smoking and mental health issues between the nations. For example, Scotland has the highest suicide rate among young men, and consumes 40 per cent more anti-depressants than England. Therefore, it is argued that services would be far more effective if more power was available locally in terms of funding, performance, governance and accountability. The New Labour government elected in 1997 stated that it would prioritize devolution and it did so successfully, transferring powers to the Scottish Parliament and Welsh Assembly on 1st July 1999 and to the Northern Ireland Assembly on 2nd December 1999.

Since devolution, each of the nations has developed slightly different structures for the design and delivery of health and social care services; *Health Boards* in Scotland and Wales, PCTs and now CCGs in England, and integrated *Health and Social Care Trusts* in Northern Ireland. These different structural forms clearly have implications for how inter-agency working happens in practice within these different arrangements. A number of 'flagship' policy ideas have also emerged, which mark clear policy differences in terms of the devolved nations: for example, Scotland and its free personal care (Dickinson *et al.*, 2007), Wales and its free prescriptions and parking in hospitals or Northern Ireland and its more integrated structures. Yet, on the whole, a number of the ultimate aims and ends of policy have remained fairly consistent. There is much debate in the literature about the degree to which devolution will open up to greater policy divergence or whether after an initial period there will be convergence once more (Jeffrey, 2007).

Greer (2008) argues that devolution and the structural changes that have occurred as part of this process have impacted on the *cultures* of health care systems across the four nations:

- **Scotland** is characterized by *professionalism* given its relatively flat organizational structure and the high status of medical leaders who are closely connected with policy.
- **England** is characterized in terms of *markets and managerialism* with its processes of *market*-based reform such as FTs, Payment by Results and so forth, and its reliance on managers to help drive change.
- **Wales** introduced a number of changes after devolution seeking to *localize* services as far as possible, although in more recent years this process has been reversed again with the *merger* of *Health Boards*. Much of the language surrounding Welsh health care is communitarian and there is a rejection of the sorts of market-based reforms embraced in England.
- **Northern Ireland** can be characterized by its *permissive managerialism*. Given the political situation, Northern Ireland has often had little control over its health policy due to long periods of direct control. The system has been fairly stable and managers have been given a high degree of autonomy over services.

As this illustrates, aside from individual policies, there are a number of more profound differences within the health and social care systems of the four nations, all of which have implications in terms of joint working.

Recommendations for policy and practice

- Different national, regional or local areas may face different types of challenges and it may therefore be helpful for them to have more power and responsibility in terms of leading and shaping their services.
- Devolution has led to some quite different structures across the four nations, which have different implications in terms of the opportunities and challenges of joint working.
- This may give an opportunity to share common problems and lessons learned across four increasingly different contexts.
- Although some 'flagship' policies have changed across the devolved nations, a number of the aims of policy have remained the same.
- However, structural changes are not the only significant issue and profound differences in the cultures of these systems have also emerged.

KEY TEXTS

- Connolly, S., Bevan, G. and Mays, N. (2010) *Funding and Performance of Healthcare Systems in the Four Countries of the UK Before and After Devolution* (London: The Nuffield Trust)

  This offers an overview of the history of political devolution and an account of the experience of funding and performance of the four health care systems.

- Greer, S.L. (2008) 'Devolution and Divergence in UK Health Policies', *British Medical Journal*, 337: p. a2616

  This reviews health policy in the devolved nations and discusses the degree to which this has led in divergence in terms of their policies and culture.

- National Audit Office (2012) *Healthcare Across the UK: A Comparison of the NHS in England, Scotland, Wales and Northern Ireland* (London: TSO)

  National study identifying key trends and variations across the four nations of the United Kingdom.

disability

SEE **physical disability; social model**

e

elected members

SEE local government

evaluation

SEE ALSO theory

At its most simple, evaluation is the 'process of determining the merit, worth or value of something, or the produce of that process' (Scriven, 1991, p. 139). Evaluation then is something we all do on a daily basis in going about our everyday lives. This is a fairly broad term and so in the context of social sciences has been described as a family of research methods that involves the 'systematic application of social research procedures in assessing the conceptualization and design, implementation, and utility of social intervention programs. In other words, evaluation research involves the use of social research methodologies to judge and improve the planning, monitoring, effectiveness and efficiency of health, education, welfare and other human service programs' (Rossi and Freeman, 1985, p. 19).

In the context of inter-agency working, evaluation therefore involves selecting a particular investigative approach that examines some part (or parts) of the processes and/or outcomes of collaborative working and making some judgements as to the worth or value of this. Within the wider literature, there are a number of different evaluations of inter-agency working (see Dickinson, 2008 for a summary). However, these often tend to focus much more on the processes of inter-agency working than on the outcomes. This means that evaluators have a tendency to look at how partners are working together and what the major barriers and facilitators of this are – rather than whether this makes any difference to the kinds of services that are provided or indeed the service user outcomes this might produce.

In thinking about evaluation, it is helpful to distinguish between inputs, outputs and outcomes. The first of these – inputs – are the resources (be that human, material or financial) that are used to carry out activities and produce or accomplish results. Outputs refer to the effects of a process (such as a service) on an administrative structure (Axford and Berry, 2005). They are the direct products or services that stem from the activities of initiatives and are delivered to a specific group or population. Outcomes are the 'impact, effect or consequences of help received' (Nicholas *et al.*, 2003, p. 2). That is, outcomes are not just the direct products or services, but are the totality of the consequences of the actions of an organization, policy, programme or initiative. In other words outcomes are the 'impact on society of a particular public sector activity' (Smith, 1996, p. 1).

Traditionally health and social care tended to be performance managed on the basis of outputs rather than outcomes. So they would often be more concerned with, for example, how many people have accessed a particular service and not necessarily the difference that this intervention made or the quality of that intervention. However, with the influence of *New Public Management* (NPM) and pressures from service users calling for better quality of services in recent years we have seen much more of a call to measure services by outcome rather than by output. In the case of inter-agency working, there is little evidence that shows a clear link between collaborative working and improved service user outcomes (Dickinson, 2008). However, it is important to note that there are limited numbers of outcome evaluations of inter-agency working and being able to effectively evaluate collaborative working is very difficult for a range of reasons (e.g. timescales, attributing change to joint working initiatives etc). If you are conducting an outcome evaluation, one of the issues that needs to be clear from the outset is just what outcomes you are trying to deliver. Otherwise it can be very difficult to come to valid conclusions about the degree to which these have been achieved.

In addition to distinguishing between inputs, outputs and outcomes, the evaluation literature has also seen a growing trend towards theory-led approaches to evaluating public services. Theory-led approaches such as realistic evaluation (Pawson and Tilley, 1997) and theories of change (Connell *et al.*, 1995) are often seen in contrast to method-led approaches. Method-led approaches aim at refining the use of particular approaches (methods) with the aim that this should reveal insight into particular initiatives. Such a perspective suggests that if we use the right method to investigate an issue or policy, then we should be able to get to the truth. Theory-led approaches instead aim at mapping out the series of assumptions (or programme theories) underpinning a particular imitative and then to test different aspects of this. So, for example, in the context of inter-agency working, a theory-based approach would map out what is happening in terms of efforts to work jointly and what impacts this should produce on the partner agencies, services and outcomes. Once this has been mapped out, then different aspects of this would be tested using a range of approaches.

Recommendations for policy and practice
- Inter-agency working can be very difficult to evaluate in practice and careful thought needs to be given to this process.
- There are many different possible ways to evaluate inter-agency working and so you need to be clear about what you are trying to evaluate and why to ensure that you select the most appropriate approach.
- Whichever evaluative approach is adopted, trade-offs will need to be made and these need to be acknowledged.
- It is crucial that attempts at inter-agency working are clear what outcomes they are trying to deliver if they are to be evaluated in terms of their outcomes.
- Theory-led approaches offer a lot of potential in terms of evaluating inter-agency working.

KEY TEXTS
- Barnes M. *et al.* (2005) *Health Action Zones: Partnerships for Health Equity* (London: Routledge)

  This book provides a helpful insight into the challenges of investigating joint working initiatives and making judgements about their impact using theory-based approaches.
- Dickinson H. (2008) *Evaluating Outcomes in Health and Social Care* (Bristol: The Policy Press)

  This book provides a review of many of the issues involved in evaluating inter-agency working on terms of outcomes.

- Glendinning C. *et al.* (2006) *Outcomes-Focused Services for Older People* (London: SCIE)

  This report investigates the types of outcomes that older people value.

f

Foundation Trusts

SEE ALSO accountability; acute care; community services; governance;
mixed economy of care

In England, the creation of an internal market in the early 1990s saw
hospitals become self-managing 'NHS Trusts', with Boards based
on private sector models and a business model based around NHS
commissioners purchasing their services. In practice, there was relatively little competition (especially in some part of the country) and
hospitals remained very powerful organizations, often able to resist
the desire of some commissioners for more radical service redesign. From 2003, high-performing Trusts were strengthened yet
further with the advent of Foundation status (under the Health and
Social Care (Community Health and Standards) Act 2003). Under
this new model, hospitals could apply to a new regulator, Monitor,
to become FTs: legally independent organizations or Public Benefit
Corporations no longer subject to direction from the Secretary of
State. They not only have a Board similar to a non-FT, but also have
a Council of Governors made up of people chosen by partner agencies and elected from patients, staff and local people. They also have
a 'membership', with local people, patients and staff able to become
a member of the Trust and, in principle, become more involved in
the life of the hospital (see Ham and Hunt, 2008 for an early study
into FT membership).

  In practice, some FTs have seemed unsure how best to work with
their members, and the exact benefit of membership can sometimes
remain slightly obscure. More recently, Foundation status has since
been extended to *Mental Health* Trusts and to some *community services*. Over time, different governments have expressed the desire for
all *acute* and mental health Trusts to be FTs, with various deadlines
(all missed to date) for this to happen. In practice, this has been
difficult – as some hospitals seem to have long-term financial and/

or structural problems and may ultimately be non-viable (and hence will not meet the thresholds required to achieve Foundation status). Whether they are supported to improve over time or disbanded and their services taken on by other FTs remains to be seen – but the need for a clear stance on hospitals unlikely ever to make FT status still seems important.

Recommendations for policy and practice
- Giving greater freedom and power to high-performing acute trusts now feels a policy very much focused on the desire of New Labour to tackle waiting times and to improve productivity in hospitals. With hindsight, it may have made some of more recent attempts to shift care closer to home even more difficult.
- FTs seem to be performing better than non-FTs in some respects – but this seems to be the result of longstanding differences and not the result of the FT policy itself. However, over time FTs may be becoming more business-like in their approach.
- While membership and governorship have the potential to improve relationships and local accountability, a number of FTs seem to have struggled to know how to do this well – and parts of this agenda still feel under-developed. Certainly, FTs do not feel significantly more genuinely locally democratic as a result of this approach.
- Improving the accountability of providers rather than of commissioners feels slightly contradictory at a time when successive governments are promoting more commissioning-based approaches.
- Some FTs seem to have been able to generate surpluses. Whether this is prudent planning ahead or a waste of resources that could be being spent in the here and now probably depends on your point of view.

KEY TEXTS
- Allen, P. *et al.* (2011) *Investigating the Governance of NHS Foundation Trusts* (NIHR: SDO programme) (project 08/1618/157)

  In-depth study of governance in four FTs to explore internal and external governance.

- Exworthy, M., Frosini, F. and Jones, L. (2011) 'Are NHS Foundation Trusts Able and Willing to Exercise Autonomy? "You Can Take a Horse to Water ... "', *Journal of Health Services Research and Policy*, 16 (4): pp. 232–237

  Essay exploring the extent to which FTs feel able to exercise autonomy and the reasons why not.

- Ham, C. and Hunt, P. (2008) *Membership Governance in NHS Foundation Trusts: A Review for the Department of Health* (Birmingham/ London: Health Services Management Centre/Mutuo)

  Early study into membership of FTs.

g

General Practice

SEE Clinical Commissioning Groups; primary care

governance

SEE ALSO accountability; devolution; New Public Management

Governance is a broad topic and one that has received substantial interest over the past thirty years or so – although the meaning of this term is far from straight forward. As Newman (2001, p. 12) highlights, 'governance has become a rather promiscuous concept, linked to a range of theoretical perspectives and policy approaches.' Governance acts as a 'descriptive and normative term, referring to the way in which organisations and institutions are (or should be) governed' (p. 16). Although definitions of governance vary, most contain common themes such as those of direction, control, *values* and *accountability*.

The issue of corporate governance is the one that we have heard much about in the media from the scandals of the 1980s and 1990s (e.g. World Corp, Enron, Arthur Anderson etc.) up to the more recent banking crisis. Since this time governments have focused on encouraging organizations to achieve 'good corporate governance', although what 'good' governance means is often less than clear. Good governance is often advocated on the basis that it should lead to better organizational performance, although the evidence to support this is limited. From a review of the literature, Skelcher *et al.* (2004) conclude, 'the theoretical connections between govern-ance arrangements and organisational performance are poorly supported by empirical evidence' (p. 14).

However, it is not just a concern with corporate scandals that has focused attention on governance. Lynn *et al.* (2001) argue that this recent emphasis on governance is due to public policies increasingly being delivered: 'through complicated webs of states, regions...non-profit organizations, collaborations, networks, partnerships and other means for the control and coordination of dispersed activities' (p. 1). The impacts of reforms associated with New Public Management philosophies and the separation of purchasers and providers of health and social care, along with the increased use of different types of public, private and third sector organizations to deliver these services, mean that governance has become important as a way of 'steering' communities.

At the core of these sorts of arguments is the idea that the role of government in its wider sense has changed. As Newman explains, 'governance theory starts from the proposition that we are witnessing a shift from government (through direct control) to governance (through steering, influencing, and collaborating with multiple actors in a dispersed system)...The state, it is argued, can no longer assume a monopoly of expertise or resources necessary to govern, and must look to a plurality of inter-dependent institutions drawn from the public, private and voluntary sectors' (2001, p. 71). In the organizational theory literature, it is suggested that there are three primary modes of governance through which partners might interact with one another: *markets, hierarchies* and *networks*. In much of the recent literature about governance, it suggests that we have moved away from governing welfare services by hierarchy to network modes.

If we think of governance in this broader sense (rather than simply corporate governance), we might understand it as a process of

- securing agreement on a programme of action among a diversity of actors/organizations;
- redistributing the capacity of actors/organizations to interpret decisions according to their own values;
- gaining acceptance that resulting actions are legitimate. (Contandripoulos *et al.*, 2004)

As such, Peck and Dickinson (2008, p. 60) define governance in the context of inter-agency settings as the 'mechanisms that legitimise authority, accountability, policies and procedures in organisations – or in the relationships between organisations – within the social and political environment in which they operate.' Peck and Dickinson go on to argue that good governance has to both *deliver legitimacy* (by engaging the appropriate range of stakeholders) and *perform legitimacy* (by building cohesion and commitment). Poor governance will do neither.

There is limited evidence concerning the instrumental value that systems of governance play (e.g. the degree to which Boards actually take difficult decisions or whether they primarily 'rubber stamp' decisions elsewhere). However, Boards (particularly those operating in an inter-agency context) may not actually be redundant but play an important *symbolic role* – for example, by demonstrating how seriously partner agencies take the issue of joint working and how much senior sign up there is. Equally, symbolism can sometimes be bad – for example if a 'Partnership Board' chose to meet in the local authority Council Chambers, with a local authority chair, local authority minute-takers and using local authority processes and paperwork this might give a symbolic message to NHS colleagues that this isn't necessarily a fully joint agenda. As Skelcher *et al.* (2004) conclude, 'it is easier to establish the implications of governance arrangements for democratic performance than for organisational performance' (p. 14). In other words, it is easier to show that a specific form of governance has contributed to symbolic performance (such as being seen to be legitimate) than it has to instrumental performance (such as actually achieving targets).

Recommendations for policy and practice
- Be clear when you are discussing governance with organizational partners that you are all talking about the same thing.
- Be realistic about the limits of the instrumental impact of your governance arrangements.
- Be aware of the potential – both positive but also negative – of the symbolic impact of these arrangements.

KEY TEXTS
- Davies, J.S. (2011) *Challenging Governance Theory: From Networks to Hegemony* (Bristol: The Policy Press)

  This provides a critical analysis of the concept of governance and its relationship to networks.

- Newman, J. (2001) *Modernising Governance: New Labour, Policy and Society* (London: Sage)

This book provides a helpful account of the meaning and history of governance and applies this particularly to the context of welfare services under New Labour.

- Skelcher, C., Mathur, N. and Smith, M. (2004) *Effective Partnership and Good Governance: Lessons for Policy and Practice* (Birmingham: Institute of Local Government Studies, University of Birmingham)

  Helpful discussion paper, including insights into the Governance Assessment Tool developed by the Institute of Local Government Studies to explore good governance locally.

h

Health Act flexibilities

SEE ALSO culture; governance; mergers and acquisitions

When New Labour were elected in 1997, an early pledge was to develop more co-ordinated services (often described as 'joined-up solutions to joined-up problems'). This happened in a number of ways (see the entry on *area-based initiatives*), but in health and social care a key element of this commitment was embodied in the 1999 Health Act. In 1998, a consultation paper on health and social care partnerships (*Partnership in Action*) gave a very hard-hitting but accurate critique of the current state of play (Department of Health, 1998, p. 3):

> All too often when people have complex needs spanning both health and social care good quality services are sacrificed for sterile arguments about boundaries. When this happens people, often the most vulnerable in our society ... and those who care for them find themselves in the no man's land between health and social services. This is not what people want or need. It places the needs of the organisation above the needs of the people they are there to serve. It is poor organisation, poor practice, poor use of taxpayers' money – it is unacceptable.

Arising out of this, the 1999 Act introduced three new powers (or 'flexibilities' as they were known): the power to create pooled health and social care budgets, to designate one partner as the lead commissioner for a particular user group and to create integrated provision. These were to be entirely voluntary, and available for use where they would help local areas work together more effectively and/or cement existing relationships. Crucially, a pooled budget involved health and social care money that was contributed to the joint pot losing its original health and social care identity so that it could be spent flexibly according to the agreement governing the pool. Lead commissioning arrangements were often used where the NHS took responsibility for *mental health* and local government took a lead on *learning disability*. Integrated provision was often used to create mental health 'partnership' Trusts, offering more joined-up health and social care. Originally known under the various sections of the 1999 Act (e.g. as a 'section 31 agreement'), these powers acquired new names under an updated NHS Act 2006 (e.g. a pooled budget was a 'section 75 agreement' under this legislation). Such powers still remain and often underpin a range of other mechanisms such as *Care Trusts*, some *Children's Trusts*, initiatives such as *intermediate care* and integrated equipment stores, and various local approaches to *joint commissioning*.

Interestingly, some of the impetus for the Health Act flexibilities appears to have come from – or at least coincided with – early developments in Somerset, which saw the creation of the United Kingdom's first integrated mental health provider and the first integrated health and social care organization in England. Although quoted as a national example of good practice in *The NHS Plan* (Department of Health, 2000) and seen as a blueprint for the Health Act and for subsequent integrated provision, an independent evaluation in 2002 produced more nuanced results – again suggesting caution about the limitations of *mergers and acquisitions* (Peck *et al.*, 2002).

In principle, the Health Act flexibilities have given local areas much more freedom to innovate. While the health and social care divide still exists, they now have greater scope to blur this boundary at local level and work together more flexibly. In practice, there were early concerns about the bureaucracy that such mechanisms sometimes entailed, with some areas feeling held back by what they saw as complex legal and audit requirements. Many organizations also felt that the broader inspection and performance management system was not very joined-up – in a worst-case scenario, joint services funded through a pooled budget felt they had no choice but to disaggregate such joint work into separate 'health' and 'social care' labels so they could feed it back up separate performance management routes. In some areas, too, a lack of trust led to very complex partnership agreements – almost so long that they seemed more like a contractual relationship than they did a genuine partnership. Although the Health Act was a major step forward, it remains difficult to work together in a context where joint working isn't necessarily embedded at every level of the system.

Recommendations for policy and practice

- Rather than insisting on wholesale reorganization, the Health Act sought to encourage more flexible collaboration at local level, leaving the health and social care divide intact but enabling local agencies to work together more flexibly.
- The advantage of such an approach is that it enables areas that want to develop their joint work to do so – but the risk is that areas that do not have a close enough relationship to make such 'flexibilities' work do not or cannot make use of such options.
- At the same time, asking local agencies to work together in an overall system that remains divided can cause friction – and a key role for future policy may be to try to remove as many barriers to joint working as possible.
- At local level, health and social care agencies wishing to use these mechanisms should ensure the early and active involvement of colleagues from audit, finance and legal services.
- Many years later, some of these flexibilities still seem a little under-utilized, and some local areas might benefit from revisiting the Health Act and the opportunities it offers.

KEY TEXTS

- Audit Commission (2009) *Means to an End: Joint Financing across Health and Social Care* (London: Audit Commission)

  National review of joint financing arrangements, including the use of section 75.

- Audit Commission (2011) *Joining up Health and Social Care: Improving Value for Money across the Interface* (London: Audit Commission)

  Broader report providing a national overview of ways in which the NHS and councils can work together to make the savings required of them.

- Glendinning, C. *et al.* (2002) *National Evaluation of Notifications for the Use of the Section 31 Partnership Flexibilities in the Health Act 1999: Final Project Report* (Leeds/Manchester: Nuffield Institute for Health/ National Primary Care Research and Development Centre)

  Early national evaluation of the Health Act, conducted by a number of leading researchers on health and social care partnerships. A similar team also conducted the national evaluation in Wales (see Young *et al.*, 2003).

Health Boards (Wales and Scotland)

SEE ALSO **devolution**

With the introduction of the *devolved* administrations for Scotland, Wales, and Northern Ireland, the policy detail and structures of health and social services are becoming increasingly diverse. While Northern Ireland has integrated *Health and Social Care Trusts*, arguably England is at the other extreme of the spectrum with a clear division between the payer (PCTs/*CCGs*) and providers (through a *mixed economy* of care). Wales and Scotland both have organizational structures known as Health Boards, which are essentially responsible for the local health services of a particular geographical area – although there are slight differences between the precise features of these countries. What is consistent across these two countries, though, is that they have rejected the purchaser–provider split associated with the English NHS (and the phrase 'strategic planning' may be used more often than the more English notion of 'strategic *commissioning*').

Scotland has 14 geographically based local NHS Boards (Area Health Boards). Since the abolition of NHS Trusts, Boards have gone through internal management restructurings of varying kinds. Some have evolved into highly integrated structures, with responsibility for operational management taken by a single chief operating officer and a close-knit senior management team grouped round the chief executive and the chief operating officer. Others have delegated operational management to levels further down the hierarchy. All, however, have senior management teams who between them are responsible for the planning and delivery of the full range of health care services and for health improvement. Scottish NHS Boards are responsible for:

- implementation of the local health plan;
- resource allocation;
- performance management of the local NHS system;
- integrated health and community planning;
- regional workforce plans;
- operational management through the operating divisions.

Hospitals are managed as an acute division of the NHS Board and GPs and pharmacies are contracted through the Board. Contracted services work through Community Health Partnerships, which are largely based on local authority boundaries. Boards also have local authority nominees who have membership in order to improve the co-ordination of health and social care. In some areas, Community Health Partnerships also provide social care and these are called Community Health and Care Partnerships.

Alongside the dissolution of Trusts, Scotland developed a range of Managed *Clinical Networks* (MCNs), which typically sit at a regional level. MCNs are linked groups of health professionals and organizations from primary, secondary and tertiary care working together in a co-ordinated way (unconstrained by geographical/professional boundaries) to ensure equitable provision of clinically effective services. As Greer (2004) outlines, MCNs were partly justified by the need to use resources better, but they were also more fundamentally about attempts to harness the professions as institutions to the goals of the government (i.e. quality and value for money). In this way, MCNs are about organizing specialized services according to the needs of the population and the technical processes these services involve (i.e. networks of professionalized care), rather than by the bricks and mortar of institutions (i.e. hospitals).

Since 2009 Wales has had seven Health Boards that replaced the 22 Local Health Boards (LHBs), which it had maintained for six years previously. Not only did this reorganization create far fewer LHBs, but it also created unified organizations, which both commission and provide services. The previous 22 LHBs interfaced with the 22 local authorities that cover Wales. This number of local authorities remains today and work with the seven Health Boards to provide joined up health and social care services.

Health Boards are responsible for:

- planning;
- designing;
- developing and securing delivery of primary, community, secondary care services;
- specialist and tertiary services for their areas, to meet identified local needs within the national policy and standards framework set out by the Minister.

In 2004 the Welsh Assembly Government (WAG) published *Making the Connections*, which emphasized the role of collaboration and cooperation in bringing about improvements in public service delivery. Given the key characteristics of Wales as a small country with an absence of large metropolitan areas, but quite specific values and attitudes towards public services, the mechanisms of competition and choice that England was pursuing as drivers of reform were viewed as inappropriate. The vision of this document is clear in its intention to deliver world-class public service for the people of Wales through a process of collaboration. The Government's strategy for the NHS, *Designed for Life* (2005), similarly rejected a consumer model of reform in favour of a citizen model, and highlighted the need for the NHS to work with local government in delivering world-class services. A year later, the review of local public service delivery in Wales led by Sir Jeremy Beecham, *Beyond Boundaries* (2006), reviewed progress in implementing the citizen model, and noted that much remained to be done to make a reality of *partnership working.*

Recommendations for policy and practice
- Wales and Scotland have different structures for the delivery of health care services through Health Boards.
- What these structures have in common is that they both reject the purchaser–provider split of the English NHS.
- Both Scotland and Wales have focused on the creation of more integrated health and social care services.
- The implications of these different structures are that there are different levers and barriers to the provision of 'joined up' services between health and social care.
- Over time, devolution may create a series of natural experiments, with scope to learn more about what works when trying to deliver integrated care and what outcomes this has for local people.

KEY TEXTS
- Connolly, S., Bevan, G. and Mays, N. (2010) *Funding and Performance of Healthcare Systems in the Four Countries of the UK Before and After Devolution* (London: The Nuffield Trust)

  This offers an overview of the history of political devolution and an account of the experience of funding and performance of the four health care systems.

- Greer, S. (2008) 'Devolution and Divergence in UK Health Policies', *British Medical Journal,* 337: a2616

  This paper reviews health policy in the devolved nation and discusses the degree to which this has led in divergence in terms of their policies and culture.

- National Audit Office (2012) *Healthcare across the UK: A Comparison of the NHS in England, Scotland, Wales and Northern Ireland* (London: TSO)

health scrutiny

SEE **local government**

Health and Social Care Trusts (Northern Ireland)

SEE ALSO **Care Trusts; devolution; mergers and acquisitions**

In recent years Scottish and Welsh health services have become increasingly divergent to that of England as the *devolution* of powers has led to different decisions being taken about the structure and organization of these services.

Northern Ireland, however, has perhaps a greater pedigree in this sense having had integrated health and social care services since 1973. Heenan and Birrell (2006, p. 48) argue that the Northern Ireland system is 'one of the most structurally integrated and comprehensive models of health and personal social services in Europe.' However, this system was not created because of clear evidence about the efficacy of integrated care services – social services were removed from local government in 1973 due to a 'political imperative created by the failure of local government' (Heenan and Birrell, 2006, p. 64) and health and social care were administered by four integrated health and social services boards. There have been a number of reorganizations of boundaries and organizational functions since this time (Taylor, 2011), but integrated management arrangements for both children's and adult's services have remained.

While Scotland and Wales have had a strong emphasis on the localization of services since devolution, Northern Ireland has a much more centralized system. Today Northern Ireland has a total of five

Health and Social Care Trusts, which provide integrated health and social care services (and an additional Ambulance Trust):

- Belfast Health and Social Care Trust,
- South Eastern Health and Social Care Trust,
- Northern Health and Social Care Trust,
- Southern Health and Social Care Trust,
- Western Health and Social Care Trust,
- Northern Ireland Ambulance Service Trust.

These Trusts were created following the amalgamation of a number of smaller Trusts so that they cover much larger areas then previously. Health and Social Care Trusts manage and administer hospitals, health centres, residential homes, day centres and other health and social care facilities and provide a wide range of health and social care services to the community. These Trusts are commissioned by a centralized and integrated commissioning board.

In the late 1990s and early 2000s, Northern Ireland's integrated health and social care system was much vaunted and was commended by the Health Select Committee (1996) and the Royal Commission on Long Term Care (1999). Yet, as Heenan and Birrell (2006, p. 48) note, 'to date, the arrangements in Northern Ireland have been the subject of very scant research attention.' These authors go on to quote Richards (2000), who has described this situation as 'amazing' and 'difficult to explain' – but even since this time few attempts have been made to investigate these structures in more detail (with the exception of the works of Heenan and Birrell).

In 2006 Heenan and Birrell concluded that 'the most distinctive feature of integration are that all professionals are employed by the same organisation, have the same source of funding, share the same goals and objective and work alongside each other' (p. 62). However, they did identify challenges with the system and argued that more research was needed in order to be able to make statements about the impacts that this has had on patients. These findings were echoed by Reilly *et al.* (2007) who concluded that the structures of integrated services in Northern Ireland are more conducive to joint working, but that these are not in themselves sufficient to produce integrated practice or ensure better service outcomes.

Heenan and Birrell (2009) go on to suggest that the Northern Ireland system has seen achievements in terms of reducing delayed discharges, investing in new services (e.g. integrated care teams) and improved referral and assessment. However, they do find difficulties with the integrated care system. The primary among these is the tendency of health to dominate the agenda at the expense of social care *values* and priorities. Much of the new resource and the media and public profile tends to be around the acute sector, meaning that little priority is given to the preventative agenda. Heenan and Birrell (2009) conclude that integration has not reached its full potential and that what is needed to do this is:

- a higher profile for social care in the modernization initiative;
- joint initial training sessions for health and social care professionals;
- a focus on outcomes for service users;
- a renewed debate on *social models* of care;
- the composition of the new bodies to reflect a more equal status between health and social care;
- a systematic programme of research and evaluation around integrated working to provide a robust evidence base.

Recommendations for policy and practice
- Northern Ireland has had an integrated health and social care system since 1973 and as such offers a helpful example that we might draw on for experience and evidence of integrated care.
- The integrated care arrangements were not, however, introduced due to clear evidence that integrated care is more effective but due to concerns over the effectiveness of local government.
- There is limited research evidence to report on the Northern Ireland experience, but what there is suggests that the experience is not all positive and integrated working can bring disbenefits as well as advantages.
- One of the positives of the integrated health and care system is that there is one employer, one vision and set of values and therefore less incentive to pass the buck to partners.
- One of the negatives of the integrated care system is that health has a tendency to dominate the agenda.

KEY TEXTS

- Heenan, D. and Birrell, D. (2006) 'The Integration of Health and Social Care: The Lessons from Northern Ireland', *Social Policy and Administration*, 40: pp. 47–66

  This journal article reports empirical research into the experience of integration in Northern Ireland.

- Heenan, D. and Birrell, D. (2009) 'Organisational Integration in Health and Social Care: Some Reflections on the Northern Ireland Experience', *Journal of Integrated Care*, 17 (5): pp. 3–12

  Journal article exploring the practical implications of integrated care in Northern Ireland.

- National Audit Office (2012) *Healthcare across the UK: A Comparison of the NHS in England, Scotland, Wales and Northern Ireland* (London: TSO)

Health and Well-Being Boards

SEE ALSO **area-based initiatives; Clinical Commissioning Groups; governance; joint commissioning; Joint Strategic Needs Assessment; leadership; local government; public health**

Following the creation of a Conservative–Liberal Democrat coalition in 2010, the *Liberating the NHS* White Paper set out a series of reforms (Department of Health, 2010a) later enacted in the Health and Social Care Act 2012. Although the bulk of the White Paper focused on changes within the NHS (and in particular on *clinical commissioning*), a key theme of the paper was also about creating greater local *accountability*. As part of a broader 'localism' agenda, a key mechanism is the Health and Well-Being Board, described in the White Paper in the following terms (p. 34):

> The Government will strengthen the local democratic legitimacy of the NHS. Building on the power of the local authority to promote local wellbeing, we will establish new statutory arrangements within local authorities – which will be established as 'health and wellbeing boards' or within existing strategic partnerships – to take on the function of joining up the commissioning of local NHS services, social care and health improvement. These health and wellbeing boards allow local

authorities to take a strategic approach and promote integration across health and adult social care, children's services, including safeguarding, and the wider local authority agenda.

Going live in April 2013, Health and Well-Being Boards bring together *CCGs* and the local Council to carry out the annual *Joint Strategic Needs Assessment* (JSNA) and develop a local Health and Well-being Strategy. They are likely to be a key forum for future *joint commissioning* and the use of existing mechanisms such as the *Health Act flexibilities*. They may also be a natural forum to provide an overview of the changes taking place in *public health*. They should include at least one local Councillor, a representative of Healthwatch (see the entry on *involvement*), a representative of each CCG, the Directors of Adult Social Services and of Children's Services and the Director of Public Health.

Although it remains early days, there may well be lessons from the *governance* structures of previous *area-based initiatives* (including previous Local Strategic Partnerships). Given there is sometimes a local sense that some of these forums became little more than 'talking shops' in some parts of the country, a key challenge for Health and Well-Being Boards will be to reflect on previous attempts at creating strategic partnership boards and about ways in which current arrangements will need to be different in order to achieve desired outcomes.

Recommendations for policy and practice
- Health and Well-Being Boards have a crucial role to play in providing whole systems leadership and preventing fragmentation within the system.
- However, this role is difficult to articulate or to capture in formal governance structures. In one way, it might best be described as a role around 'sensemaking' – having the key people in the same room to jointly receive national policy, make sense of it for the local context and help translate this for each local organization.
- With this in mind, local areas need to decide what they are trying to achieve together and what kind of Health and Well-being Board they might need as a result. The danger is that in the rush to establish such Boards the debate is more about membership, reporting and governance, rather than about desired outcomes.

- Although Health and Well-Being Boards will bring together a range of different stakeholders, a key relationship in the current context will be between lead GPs and local councillors – both of whom are often key local figures with lots of local knowledge and who often stay in the same area for much longer than NHS or social care managers. How these two groups work together could be crucial.
- Whatever happens, there is some helpful learning from previous area-based initiatives, and it will be important not to re-invent the wheel.

KEY TEXTS

- Humphries, R. *et al.* (2012) *Health and Wellbeing Boards: System Leaders or Talking Shops?* (London: King's Fund)

  Helpful policy commentary based on survey of 50 local authorities.

- NHS Confederation and partners (2011) *Operating Principles for Health and Well-Being Boards: Laying the Foundations for Healthier Places* (London: NHS Confederation)

  Early guidance from key health and local government national bodies.

- Wistow, G. (2011) *Integration This Time? Liberating the NHS and the Role of Local Government* (London: Local Government Association)

  Policy paper exploring the history of joint working between the NHS and local government and a series of key lessons/principles relevant for current reforms.

hierarchies

SEE ALSO **markets; networks**

Traditional organizational theory suggests that there are three primary ways that organizations interact with one another: through hierarchies, *markets* or *networks*. Each of these different modes is characterized in a number of different ways, such as what factors link partners, how they communicate, how flexible these arrangements are and how they resolve conflict (see Table 1). Often these ways of interacting are set in contrast to one another and they are seen as distinct ways of organizing – although in reality modes might be settlements of these ideal types. In this section we provide an overview of hierarchies,

	Market	*Hierarchy*	*Network*
Normative basis	Contract	Employment relationship	Complementary strengths
Means of communication	Prices	Routines	Relational
Methods of conflict resolution	Haggling – resort to courts	Administrative fiat – supervision	Norm of reciprocity – reputational concerns
Degree of flexibility	High	Low	Medium
Amount of commitment among the parties	Low	Medium	High
Tone or climate	Precision and/or suspicion	Formal, bureaucratic	Open-ended, mutual benefits
Actor preferences or choices	Independent	Dependent	Interdependent

TABLE I   *Modes of governance and characteristics*
Source: Lowndes and Skelcher (1998, p. 319).

but readers may also find it helpful to read entries on markets and networks to get a complete picture of these concepts.

Williamson (1975) provided one of the first attempts to differentiate between different modes of governance writing from a perspective of Transaction Cost Economics (TCE). TCE suggests that where individuals or organizations have partially overlapping goals they are forced to cooperate. The process of collaboration will only occur, therefore, if it is in the mutual interest of each party to try control or influence the other's activities. Cooperation requires interdependence, which calls for some form of transaction or exchange, where each individual gives something of value (e.g. labour) and receives something of value in return (e.g. money).

A hierarchy is essentially a structure where a single individual or group sits at the top and holds power, with different layers of authority below this. Actions and interactions between actors in a hierarchical organization are guided by the *power* that one actor holds over another. This differs from a market (where interactions are mediated by a price mechanism where resource changes hands between actors) and networks (which are typically guided by trust).

Markets are often advocated on the basis that they are more efficient than hierarchies (as hierarchical forms are often characterized as being large, unwieldy and inflexible). Yet Williamson (1975) observed that where it is difficult to establish the exact price of a good, or the transaction costs become too high, a hierarchy may be more efficient in mediating economic transactions between its members at a lower cost. In a hierarchy, each party contributes labour to the corporate body, which places a value on this and compensates it fairly. As the corporate body is trusted to mediate this relationship, transaction costs are lower, overcoming some of the difficulties markets have with collaboration. Nonetheless, because of their formalization and routine, lower transaction costs tend to come at the price of flexibility.

The UK public sector, like most public sectors, has tended to be dominated by hierarchical organizations. As Glasby and Dickinson (2008) argue, at the establishment of the welfare state, large government departments were responsible for a series of (often quite separate) welfare services, each with their own regional and local delivery structures. Authority in such a system was largely top-down, with staff at ground level reporting up to a lead officer, who in turn would report upwards. Within this context, collaboration has been seen as an important mechanism in co-ordinating the activities of welfare organizations. Various mechanisms have been introduced over time as a way of overcoming the chasms between agencies. During the New Labour governments of 1997–2010, much of the rhetoric behind these initiatives was that these were an attempt at a shift away from hierarchical and market-based forms of governance to one based on networks. However, Peck and Dickinson (2008) argue that in practice most collaboration in English health and social care has remained between hierarchical organizations. As evidence of the dominance of hierarchical forms, an example frequently given is of the *Care Trust* model, which effectively *merges* health and social care into one organizational form.

Recommendations for policy and practice
- There are three ideal forms of mediating relationships between agencies – hierarchies, markets and networks.
- Hierarchies are the most familiar of these forms to a public sector context, where *power* is centralized and there is a clear sense of formal *accountabilities*.
- Hierarchies are seen as good ways to mediate some relationships as they are relatively predictable, stable and may in some circumstances be cheap ways of organizing.
- Critics of hierarchies suggest that they are large, unwieldy and inflexible.
- Although much policy rhetoric suggests that health and social care have moved towards a network form of *governance*, much of the research evidence suggests that the hierarchy pervades.

KEY TEXTS
- Glasby, J. and Dickinson, H. (2008) *Partnership Working in Health and Social Care* (Bristol: The Policy Press)

  This text provides an overview of these concepts and applies them to an English health and social care context.

- Sullivan, H. and Skelcher, C. (2002) *Working across Boundaries: Collaboration in Public Services* (Basingstoke: Palgrave Macmillan)

  This text provides a comprehensive introduction to the various theoretical underpinnings of collaboration.

- Williamson, O.E. (1975) *Markets and Hierarchies: Analysis and Antitrust Implications* (New York: Free Press)

  This is the original text that set out the distinction between different modes of organizing.

hospital discharge

SEE ALSO **acute care; intermediate care; long-term care; older people**

Of all the fault lines between health and social care in the United Kingdom (and indeed in many other developed countries too), the issue of hospital discharge is one of the most controversial and longstanding. Whenever someone likely to have ongoing needs (often a frail *older person* or someone with multiple *long-term conditions*) is nearing discharge, they can often feel too well for hospital but not well enough to be home without support (either temporary as they regain their confidence or ongoing). This can sometimes be described as a 'discharge' from hospital (where the hospital's responsibility ends when they person is medically ready to leave). However, more recently (and more accurately) policy makers have begun to describe it as a 'transfer of care' (to reflect the fact that the person may have ongoing needs that should now be met in the community). Thus, hospital discharge – or transfers of care – require careful co-ordination, planning and joint implementation between hospital and community and between health and social care. As Henwood (1994, p. 1) suggested as far back as 1994:

> Effective hospital discharge is dependent upon the various agencies involved acknowledging their complementary responsibilities. The benefits of getting it right can include maximizing individuals' chance of recovery; improved hospital bed usage; more effective targeting of scarce assessment skills, and well informed community health staff knowing exactly what contribution they need to make to the care of the individual. The costs of getting it wrong include: a poor service to patients, and unnecessarily slow recovery; GPs not knowing what has happened to their patients; social services staff receiving inappropriate referrals; disputes breaking out; un-planned readmissions, a general waste of resources, and the risk of bad publicity on bed blocking. [Despite our traditional focus on hospital 'discharge']…it is also apparent that a discharge from hospital is an admission – or transfer – to community care; and an admission to hospital is a transfer from the community. It is crucial, therefore, to recognize that actions and decisions made at any point in a care episode can have consequences for other parts of the health and social care system.

In the same way, the term 'delayed transfers of care' describes people who are not discharged in a timely manner. Although still used in practice, terms such as 'bed blocker' are no longer felt appropriate, as they are often used pejoratively and imply that it is somehow the person's fault they are delayed in hospital rather than the fault of the system.

One of the major problems with hospital discharge is that hospital and community services often have different notions of what constitutes good practice. Thus, hospitals tend to be motivated in part by efficiency (getting a person in, treating them and discharging them as quickly as possible so as to free up the bed for a new patient who needs it more). In contrast, community social care is responsible for working with people when they are potentially at their most vulnerable and disorientated to help them make difficult but crucial decisions about their long-term future (a model based more around choice and empowerment). Arguably neither of these approaches is either right or wrong – they are just different. However, they frequently come into tension when the hospital feels someone is well enough to go home and community services want to take time to help the person decide what they want to happen and to plan the transfer well.

Although there have been a range of different policies and initiatives over time, the difficulty of planning and co-ordinating transfers of care probably dates back to the beginning of the NHS and has been recognized as a key issue at different times in the NHS's history (see Glasby, 2003 for a summary). In particular, the research evidence over time suggests that hospital discharge can all too often be characterized by poor inter-agency communication, lack of adequate planning for discharge, a failure to communicate properly with the patient and their family, insufficient notice of discharge, a tendency to take family members for granted and poorly planned/delayed community services. Although the policy focus has often been on trying to eradicate delayed transfers, moreover, the issues of poorly planned and/or premature discharge seem just as crucial (if not more so).

In England, a key – but contested – measure to tackle these problems was introduced under the Community Care (Delayed Discharge etc) Act 2003 (see Henwood, 2004, 2006 for further discussion). Under this legislation, hospitals could 'fine' social services if a patient was delayed inappropriately in hospital beyond a certain time limit for social care reasons only (a system known as 'reimbursement'). At the time, this measure attracted significant debate – with some commentators suggesting that this was a helpful way of incentivizing timely discharge and others claiming that this unfairly penalized one partner for a whole systems problem. Certainly, most local data collection has always seemed to suggest that delays can be caused by a range of factors – some to do with acute care, some to do with social care, some to do with factors beyond the control of health and social care at all and some a mixture of all of these. While the number of delays initially fell and while the legislation undoubtedly concentrated the mind, there remain problems and other approaches (such as additional funding and greater practice support provided by government) may have been more important. It has also proved difficult to sustain initial progress, and delays can rapidly increase in different localities at almost any time, thus re-opening these longstanding debates. For all the improvement there has been in policy and practice, hospital discharge remains contested – and too many discharges still do not proceed in a planned, timely and co-ordinated manner.

Recommendations for policy and practice
- Over time, the length of hospital stays has reduced and acute care has focused on more and more people with more complex needs. As a result, older people have been discharged 'quicker and sicker' (Neill and Williams, 1992, p. 17), with community services now supporting people with much more significant and complex needs than in the past.
- Arguably this is a good way of making best use of scarce and expensive hospital beds – but the extra pressure on the system has created even greater tension around the issue of discharge/transfers of care.
- Although the focus is often on delayed transfers, tackling poorly co-ordinated and/or premature discharge is arguably just as or even more important.
- Overall, the problematic nature of hospital discharge may ultimately be to do with competing notions of what constitutes good practice – and we still have not found a good way of making efficient use of beds while also providing people experiencing traumatic changes in their life the time and space to plan ahead (see the entry on *intermediate care* for further discussion).

- Introducing financial penalties (or incentives, depending on your point of view) can be a powerful mechanism – but can easily oversimplify a more complex situation and can also have unintended consequences.

KEY TEXTS

- Department of Health (2003b) *Discharge from Hospital: Pathway, Process and Practice* (London: Department of Health)

  Accessible, step-by-step good practice guidance.

- Glasby, J. (2003) *Hospital Discharge: Integrating Health and Social Care* (Abingdon: Radcliffe Medical Press)

  Introductory textbook summarizing policy, practice and research on hospital discharge.

- For research into the impact of the 2003 Act, see Godfrey *et al.* (2008) and McCoy *et al.* (2007).

i

informal care

SEE carers; mixed economy of care

integration

SEE partnership working

inter-agency working

SEE partnership working

inter-disciplinary working

SEE partnership working

inter-professional education

SEE ALSO trust; values

The different professions that are involved in delivering and designing health and social care services often have quite different *values* and perspectives. As such, professionals do not always entirely understand each other's views and approaches and this can cause difficulties or even confrontation when working together. Inter-professional education (IPE) has been seen as a solution to the practical difficulties associated with inter-agency working and a way of this reducing conflict between professionals. The essence of IPE is that professionals should 'learn together to work together' and this has been seen as a way to overcome ignorance and prejudice between health and social care practitioners. By learning together, it is assumed that professions will better understand each other and value what others bring to the practice of inter-agency working. In the longer run, it is thought that this might ultimately improve working relations and hence improve the quality of care and outcomes for service users.

The idea that professionals should learn together is relatively straight forward, although as Carpenter and Dickinson (2008) illustrate, there is some debate within the literature about what precisely IPE means and whether this involves different professions simply learning together or more structured interaction. IPE as a concept has a lot of face validity and seems like a good idea, but the main message from the literature is that it needs to be done well if it is to have the appropriate impact. In order to be clearer about what IPE should entail, Barr (2002, p. 23) produced a definition of IPE aims and methods, which has now become quite widely used. The components of IPE are identified as follows:

The application of principles of adult learning to interactive, group-based learning, which relates collaborative learning to collaborative practice within a coherent rationale which is informed by understanding of interpersonal, group, organizational and inter-organizational relations and processes of professionalization.

What is important about this definition is that there are active elements to this process and IPE does not just simply involve achieving economies of scale by teaching a large group made up of different professions. In recent years, IPE has become a key consideration in the training and education of health and social care professionals, and has been seen as a potential solution to help overcome a range of difficulties in inter-agency working. In one sense this has been positive, as IPE has gained recognition within a wide range of different fields. However, this also means that IPE runs the risk of being seen as all things to all people (and there are interesting parallels here with the notion of partnership itself).

One of the challenges of IPE is that it can be used in order to achieve a number of different potential outcomes. Finch (2000) suggests IPE might include purposes such as

- to '**know about**' the roles of other professional groups;
- to be able to '**work with**' the roles of other professionals, in the context of a team where each member has a clearly defined role;

- to be able to '**substitute for**' roles traditionally played by other professionals, when circumstances suggest that this would be more effective;
- to provide '*flexibility*' in career routes (moving across).

Given that IPE might have a number of different aims and objectives, it is important that we are clear what we are trying to achieve by different IPE interventions. Without this it makes it difficult for IPE to be successful. This is not to say that IPE might not be able to support improvement in all the areas that Finch outlines, but it is unlikely that any one programme would achieve such a broad range of objectives simultaneously. Clearly, the achievement of some of the above aims requires organizational change as well as education.

In terms of the degree to which IPE is effective or not, there are a range of studies that have been conducted. However, given that IPE may potentially hold a number of different aims and objectives and can take place at different times (e.g. pre-qualification, post-qualification), it is difficult to be definitive about its effectiveness. From a review of the various studies, Carpenter and Dickinson (2008) conclude that there is a lack of evidence of effectiveness of IPE, but this does not necessarily mean it is ineffective, just simply difficult to evaluate. The logistics of evaluating large pre-qualification programmes in a methodologically sound manner is a daunting task. IPE seems to be more effective in relation to the 'reaction' and 'learning' of students, but there is less evidence of impact on 'behaviour' or 'results'. However, this may be as a result of the way IPE has been evaluated and/or of the outcome indicators employed, and designers of IPE should be careful to incorporate *evaluation* into their programme so that they might capture its full effects.

Recommendations for policy and practice
- IPE can be a helpful tool in bringing different professions together and helping them to understand one another – both of which might make inter-agency working more effective.
- However, we need to be clear about what we mean in relation to IPE and what we are trying to achieve with it in practice. IPE may be used to achieve a number of different objectives so we need to be clear that stakeholders are aiming for the same outcomes.

- While IPE promises much, there is limited evidence of its effectiveness – although this may relate more to the fact that IPE is often a rather complex intervention and difficult to evaluate rather than it necessarily being ineffective. Evaluation should be built in as an important component of IPE programmes.

KEY TEXTS

- Barr, H. *et al.* (2005) *Effective Interprofessional Education: Argument, Assumption and Evidence* (Oxford: Blackwell Publishing)

  This provides an overview of the evidence about IPE and its outcomes.

- Carpenter, J. and Dickinson, H. (2008) *Interprofessional Education and Training* (Bristol: The Policy Press)

  This book provides a simple and accessible review of the IPE literature.

- Freeth, D. *et al.* (2005) *Effective Interprofessional Education: Development, Delivery and Evaluation* (Oxford: Blackwell Publishing)

  A helpful text for those thinking of designing or delivering IPE programmes.

inter-professional working

SEE **partnership working**

intermediate care

SEE ALSO **acute care; hospital discharge; long-term care; older people**

As the nature of *acute care* has changed over time, hospitals have found themselves caring for people with more complex needs and significantly increasing throughput. This has made them focus in ever greater detail on the most effective use of hospital beds – a scarce resource for which demand can sometimes outstrip supply. In the late 1990s in particular, this seemed to culminate in an annual 'winter crisis', with high-profile media reports of busy hospitals unable to admit patients to A&E because wards were full of patients unable to be discharged back to the community. While this later led to a series of policy attempts to provide 'the right care, in the right place at the right time', an early response was to develop a series of local pilot projects such as rapid response nursing teams, step-up or step-down beds in the community and additional out-of-hours support. From 2001 onwards, many of these were swept up into a broader concept of intermediate care – a range of local services designed to work with local older people in order to prevent inappropriate admissions to hospital, ensure timely *hospital discharge* and prevent premature admissions to permanent residential/nursing home placements. In many ways this is similar to more recent emphasis on concepts such as re-ablement and on measures to make acute hospitals more responsible for people's after-care in the first 30 days after discharge. Identified as a key priority in the 2001 National Service Framework for Older People (Department of Health, 2001a), intermediate care was boosted by the announcement of £900 million government funding to develop this new approach (albeit that questions remained as to how 'new' some of this funding was in reality).

Beginning as a series of relatively standalone pilots, intermediate care services had to work hard early on to develop more of a single point of access and to establish themselves as a mainstream alternative to acute care. In some areas this also involved trying to overcome opposition from some local GPs and hospital-based geriatricians, who sometimes saw this model as having the potential to deny older people access to high-quality hospital services and offering instead something of a second-class service. Of course, this was very different to what early advocates of intermediate care were trying to achieve (which was to keep older people out of hospital – where they might run the risk of a reduction in independence and of contracting a hospital-acquired infection – in situations where people did not need these services and could be maintained in the community and/or at home with short-term, intensive support).

According to a government circular (Department of Health, 2001b, p. 6), intermediate care includes services that meet all the following criteria:

- Are targeted at people who would otherwise face unnecessarily prolonged hospital stays or inappropriate admission to acute inpatient care, long-term residential care or continuing NHS inpatient care.
- Are provided on the basis of a comprehensive assessment, resulting in a structured individual care plan that involves active therapy, treatment or opportunity for recovery.

- Have a planned outcome of maximizing independence and typically enabling patients/users to resume living at home.
- Are time-limited, normally no longer than six weeks and frequently as little as one to two weeks or less.
- Involve cross-professional working, with a single assessment framework, single professional records and shared protocols.

While this model seemed to offer those older people who accessed it a good service, many intermediate care services seemed to struggle to rebalance the system as a whole, and could sometimes seem as something of a 'bolt on' to existing services. Perhaps not surprisingly, they also found it difficult to influence and change the role and approach of other services – such as admission and discharge practices in acute care, the district nursing service or local authority home care. Thus, while older people often valued the additional help they received, intermediate care did not always reduce admissions or speed up discharges in the manner intended – but could sometimes be an extra service on top of previous community and acute care. In some localities there was also a fear that some step-down beds in particular would end up 'warehousing' older people rather than focusing on rehabilitation and re-ablement, and that intermediate care beds might become just as 'blocked' as the hospital beds it sought to free up. Overall, some very positive services were probably developed – but the impact may have fallen short of the aspirations of the original policy makers and advocates of intermediate care.

Recommendations for policy and practice
- Drawing together previous pilots into a more cohesive intermediate care service or system seems a major step forward with potential to improve outcomes for older people.
- However, rebalancing the system more generally may take even more policy commitment than the £900 million set aside for intermediate care, and the risk is that some services became an 'extra' or a 'bolt on' rather than something that more fundamentally changed the nature and work of mainstream services.
- Although annual winter crises seemed to cease, this may have been as much to do with more in-depth planning and additional funding/capacity – and there is a corresponding risk that such crises reoccur in a difficult financial context.

- Developing new models of care requires significant clinical engagement and leadership – in this case, fears among some GPs and some geriatricians may have limited the uptake and effectiveness of intermediate care.
- Despite the advent of intermediate care, the need to develop a more preventative approach and to bridge the gap between hospital and the community more effectively still remains – and a series of more recent initiatives could helpfully review the lessons learned from intermediate care if they are to be more successful in achieving similar aims.

KEY TEXTS

For key national evaluations of intermediate care, see Barton *et al.* (2005) and Godfrey *et al.* (2005).

- Vaughan, B. and Lathlean, B. (1999) *Intermediate Care: Models in Practice* (London: King's Fund)

Early policy paper summarizing emerging models of service delivery.

- Wade, S. (ed.) (2003) *Intermediate Care of Older People* (London: Whurr Publications)

Practical and accessible textbook, edited by an experienced nursing lead with an interest in intermediate care.

involvement

SEE ALSO **co-production; personalization; power**

Although this book focuses on collaboration between different professions and agencies, it is also important that health and social care work collaboratively with people using services and their families. There is further discussion of this in entries on topics such as *co-production* and *personalization*, as well as broader consideration of issues such as *power*. However, both health and social care have long traditions of attempts to involve service users and patients in decisions about their own care and about services more generally. Typically, a number of different terms are used (from consultation to engagement and from empowerment to participation). Behind these different terms is a sense that health and social care professionals may have technical skills and be experts in how the system works – but it is people using services and their carers who are experts in their own lives and in what works best for them (in the context of their families, communities and individual circumstances). Thus, there is a desire – at least in principle – to create some sort of partnership of equals, whereby each party recognizes and builds on the expertise of the other. In the current policy context, this is often articulated most in relation to people with *long-term conditions*, where the concept of an 'expert patients programme' tries to capture a sense of the different expertise which different people bring to the table.

In practice, the commitment to involvement and engagement probably plays out differently in different settings. Social work has long been committed to working alongside people using services and local communities and to promoting *values* such as independence, self-determination and citizenship. Indeed, one of the criticisms of current *social care* is that has become very focused on individual care management and moved away from its traditional emphasis on community development. In contrast, the NHS has long had a commitment to what is often described as 'patient and public involvement', dating back to structures such as Community Health Councils in the 1970s. However, a common criticism is that this has sometimes felt like more of a passive form of engagement rather than a more radical sharing of power. One tool for exploring these issues is Arnstein's (1969) 'ladder of participation' – a visual representation of different levels of engagement that ranges from manipulation at the bottom rung through to citizen control at the very top.

Over time, national policy has created a series of different bodies to promote greater involvement and given health and social care a series of duties to consult and engage both people using services and the wider public. This has included Community Health Councils, Patient Advocacy and Liaison Services (PALs), Local Involvement Networks (LINks) and the most recent version – Healthwatch (which, from April 2013, is an independent consumer champion for health and social care). However, despite changing structures and names, involvement has arguably been promoted for at least three slightly different reasons, each of which implies a different value base, approach and desired outcomes (Ellins, 2012):

- A **rights-based approach** argues that individuals should be entitled to participate in decisions about their care. This is stressed in recent government slogans such as 'nothing about me without me'.

- An **instrumental approach** sees involvement as a way of improving services by tapping into the experiences of people needing health and social care.
- A **democratic approach** sees involvement as a way of developing new forms of political engagement (particularly with a decline in membership of trade unions/political parties and decreasing voter turnout in national and local elections). It is thus more about renewing democracy than it is about health and social care per se.

More cynically, there may also be instances of managers claiming to consult with service users and to be representing their views as a way of boosting support for their preconceived ideas/stances – a tactic known informally as 'playing the user card'.

Recommendations for policy and practice
- Health and social care have a legal duty to involve people in decisions about their care and about services more generally.
- However, involvement can be promoted for a complex range of reasons, and it is important to be clear about our motives and about what success would look like.
- Involvement means hearing different voices, and it is important to ensure that everyone with experience of or views about health and social care can take part.
- Certain groups may need particular support to participate on an equal footing. They are often described as 'hard to reach' – but a better term may be 'seldom heard' (which puts the onus on the system to find ways of enabling seldom heard groups to take part rather than on the individual).
- Involvement can often be portrayed as a *transfer* of power from professionals to individual service users. However, it can also be seen as a *sharing* of power, where the whole is greater than the sum of its parts.

KEY TEXTS
- Department of Health (2008) *Real Involvement: Working with People to Improve Health Services* (London: DH)

  Practical guidance on how to involve people in decisions about health care.

- Mauger, S. *et al.* (2010) *Involving Users in Commissioning Local Services* (York: Joseph Rowntree Foundation)

  Published by a leading charitable organization with a strong commitment to involvement, this combines research and good practice examples.

- Social Care Institute for Excellence (2008) *Seldom Heard: Developing Inclusive Participation in Social Care* (London: SCIE)

  Published by a leading national social care organization with a strong emphasis on user involvement, this paper explores ways of engaging seldom heard groups.

isomorphism

SEE **theory**

j

joint appointments

SEE ALSO **culture; governance; leadership**

Although health and social care often remain separate organizational entities, many localities have tried to embed joint working through the use of joint appointments. This can be at a very senior level (e.g. someone who is both PCT Chief Executive and Director of Adult Social Services), at a practice level (e.g. a jointly appointed person to lead an integrated team or an *intermediate care* project) and/or at a level somewhere in between (a joint appointment to head up a *joint commissioning* unit). Over time, one of the most common options has probably been for the local authority and the NHS to appoint a joint Director of Public Health – although the degree of jointness seems to vary in practice.

Although joint posts are increasingly common, they remain under-researched with little formal evidence about what impact they have or about what it feels like to occupy such a role. However, anecdotal evidence suggests that making a joint appointment can represent a strong symbolic statement about the intentions of partners – but that successfully fulfilling the requirements of a joint post can be demanding (if not impossible). In particular, the danger is that such posts feel as if the person is serving two large and not fully compatible masters at once, and the postholder can often find themselves pulled from pillar to post. Moreover, it can also seem as if the entirety of the relationship between the NHS and local government is vested in a small number of joint appointments, rather than these being an outward manifestation of a broader and deeper relationship. Thus, while joint appointments can help to cement relationships, they can also give false assurance that relationships are ok and mask more serious divides.

Recommendations for policy and practice
- In a divided system, making a number of key joint appointments seems a good way of trying to bridge some of the key gaps and

of making a symbolic statement about our commitment to joint working.

- However, holding such a post can sometimes be a frustrating experience, with the different agencies each wanting you to do something slightly different and not seeing you as fully 'one of us'.
- Being in a joint role probably does not promote more joined-up working by itself – and such post-holders need support to realize the potential benefits of this approach and to make their work more manageable.
- Having very senior joint appointments is sometimes seen as a way of saving on a senior salary – but the reality is often that the workload is no less and that a number of extra more junior posts are needed (thus, preventing savings from materializing in practice).
- Although many Director of Public Health posts are now joint, the degree of jointness can vary according to local context and the background and outlook of the person holding this role.

KEY TEXTS

This is an under-researched area generally – but early work by the Office for Public Management has summarized a series of local case studies and developed good practice guidance for both England and Scotland (OPM, 2001a, 2001b, 2004).

- Hunter, D. (ed.) (2008) *Perspectives on Joint Directors of Public Health appointments* (London: IDEA)

Fascinating edited collection exploring and critiquing joint roles, with many chapters written by people holding such posts.

joint commissioning

SEE ALSO **Clinical Commissioning Groups; commissioning; culture; governance; markets**

Although health and social care agencies are essentially independent of one another, the work that these agencies do often overlaps – particularly for individuals or groups with complex or chronic needs.

As such, joint working has remained an important feature of the health and social care policy context over time. At the same time that joint working has been growing in interest, so too has the role of *commissioning* in the public sector. These two important agendas have combined in the form of joint commissioning, where the reform agendas of joint working and of commissioning come together.

Joint commissioning has remained at the forefront of policy for some years now, with a legal requirement that local areas produce a *Joint Strategic Needs Assessment* and outcome-based commissioning being given increased impetus. Many of the types of processes that help joint commissioning in practice stem from the Health Act 1999, known as the *Health Act flexibilities*. These allowed organizations for the first time (legally at least) to pool budgets, appoint a lead commissioner and set up integrated provider services. Although joint commissioning is often predicated on the notion that it will improve service user outcomes, many of the policy initiatives that have been put in place in relation to joint commissioning have been structural or legal flexibilities and much of the focus has been on the processes to get this 'right', rather than about what this might actually achieve in practice.

Yet despite exhortations to do *more* and *better* joint commissioning, we know very little about what this means or what it looks like in practice. Against this background, Rummery and Glendinning (2000) remark that 'there is no universally agreed definition of joint commissioning: the term can cover a wide range of activities' (p. 18). One of the difficulties in being clear about the meaning of joint commissioning is that it is often conflated with joint working more generally. Furthermore, although some commentators have identified different levels of joint commissioning (e.g. individual, practice, regional, strategic etc.), arguably these levels could be applied to any form of commissioning. This means that it is sometimes difficult to differentiate what is unique about joint commissioning that is different to single agency commissioning or to joint working more generally; inevitably both will involve commissioners and providers of services and a range of different stakeholders.

One of the complexities that arise from a lack of a clear definition is that it is difficult to be clear about the type of impact joint commissioning has had in practice. Given that joint commissioning may take place at a range of different levels and around different populations or service user groups, it could be assumed that it might be attempting to achieve different types of outcomes in practice. Absent in the literature on joint commissioning (and indeed that on wider joint working) is a consideration of what it should be attempting to achieve in terms of *outcomes*. Although joint commissioning is often seen as a positive thing that should improve outcomes, it is less clear which outcomes and why. Joint commissioning has been seen as a way in which to produce more efficient services, more preventative services and more empowering and personalized services. As such, joint commissioning often appears as a rather uncritically accepted concept that should make services and outcomes better – with little sense of how and why this might be so. Without a clear sense of what joint commissioning is and what it should achieve in practice, there is a risk that it might lose legitimacy as an approach. The implications of this are that local organizations should be clear about what it is they are trying to achieve when engaging in joint commissioning, and that there needs to be more research that looks at outcomes and which can give us a better insight into what the impacts of joint commissioning might actually be.

Recommendations for policy and practice
- In a difficult policy and financial context, it clearly makes sense for agencies to do some things together rather than trying to do them separately.
- Many claims have been made for joint commissioning and the important role that it plays in the design and delivery of health and social care services.
- However, there is little evidence that clearly demonstrates that joint commissioning improves service user outcomes.
- Although joint commissioning has been much exhorted, there is often little clarity over what is meant by this concept or what it should achieve in practice. This may explain why there is more evidence in relation to the processes of joint commissioning, rather than the outcomes that it might produce.
- If agencies are clear from the outset what they are trying to achieve via joint commissioning, then it may make it easier to evaluate these outcomes. Just because there is a lack of evidence about joint commissioning and outcomes this does not mean we

should not do it – but we do need to be clear about the types of activities we are undertaking when doing this in practice and the types of effects we anticipate these actions to have.

KEY TEXTS

- Dickinson, H. and Nicholds, A. (2012) 'The Impact of Joint Commissioning' in J. Glasby (ed.), *Commissioning for Health and Well-being: An Introduction* (Bristol: The Policy Press)

  This chapter provides a review of the literature in relation to joint commissioning, covering definitions of this concept and the evidence of its impact.

- Dickinson, H. *et al.* (2013) *Joint Commissioning in Health and Social Care: An Exploration of Definitions, Processes, Services and Outcomes* (Birmingham: Health Services Management Centre) (for the NHS Health Service Research and Delivery programme)

  This report builds on a national evaluation of joint commissioning.

- Edwards, M. and Miller, C. (2003) *Integrating Health and Social Care and Making It Work* (London: Office for Public Management)

  Chapter 1: 'The Policy Context' explains the historical context of policy tools to promote joint commissioning.

- Hudson, B. (2010) 'Integrated Commissioning: New Context, New Dilemmas, New Solutions?' *Journal of Integrated Care*, 18: pp. 11–19

  This paper provides a review of the literature relating to joint commissioing and asks is there anything different about this within the contemporary context.

Joint Future (Scotland)

SEE ALSO **devolution; governance**

The notion of health and social care working jointly has a significant history in a Scottish context (for an overview see Petch, 2008a), but received increased impetus in late 1999 when the Joint Future Group was established by the Minister for Health and Community Care. The ultimate aim of this group was to 'improve joint working in order to deliver modern and effective person-centred services' (Scottish Executive, 2000, p. 54). Prior to this, *Modernising*

Community Care: An Action Plan (Scottish Office, 1998) had set out the policy priorities for joint working between health and social care in Scotland. The Joint Future Group aimed at building on the principles that had been articulated in the previous plan and at delivering against four main aims:

- to agree a list of joint measures which agencies need to have in place to deliver effective services, and to set deadlines;
- to advise on the balance between residential and home-based care;
- to advise on options for charging for care at home;
- to advise on how to identify and share good practice.

Research was commissioned into joint working in Scotland, which sought to assist the Group in being able to advise against these points (e.g. Stewart *et al.*, 2003). The Joint Future Group reported in December 2000 with a range of policy measures and 19 recommendations grouped around five core themes:

- rebalancing care of older people;
- improving joint working;
- planning, financial and service management frameworks;
- charging;
- good practice.

All of the recommendations made by the Group were endorsed by the Scottish Executive (2001) with the exception of that relating to free home care for older people, which was referred to another Group and was incorporated into the free personal care policy implemented by the Scottish Parliament in early 2001. To take the recommendations forward, the former Community Care Implementation Unit was transformed into the Joint Future Unit. A series of pilots and high-profile initiatives followed, as did the revision of many deadlines, targets and a shift in emphases. In 2004, the Joint Improvement Team was established to support health and social care partnerships. With a relatively small pool of staff, this team drew on external sources to act as both a knowledge bank in relation to joint working and also to support local level joint working.

As Petch (2008a, p. 73) notes, 'perhaps surprisingly, there has been no systematic evaluation of the impact of the Joint Future initiatives, whether at service level in terms of models of working or inter-professional relationships, or at the individual level in terms of user and carer outcomes. Any appraisal therefore has to rely on a more disparate mix of modest empirical evidence, operational wisdom, and observed practice.' Petch refers to a range of different forms of evidences in determining her perspective of the relative merits of the process. She points to the fact that joint working on this level required somewhat of a mind set and this took time to introduce. Petch argues that a number of things have been achieved on the journey to better joint working, but that this needs to be embarked on with a long-term view in mind. She also warns against the temptation of becoming focused on process over outcome, suggesting that at times the Joint Future agenda became the means rather than a means to an end.

Recommendations for policy and practice
- The Joint Future Group was established by the Scottish Executive as a way of making sense of the context of joint working in this specific national setting.
- The Joint Future Group made a series of recommendations in relation to core areas of joint working, many of which would be very similar to those found in other national contexts.
- No formalized evaluation was conducted of the Joint Future process, so it is difficult to be definitive about its impact.
- However, the initial activity was perceived by some to run the risk of focusing on process rather than outcomes.
- As other entries in this book suggest, this can be a key limitation of policy and practice around joint working.

KEY TEXTS
- Hudson, B. (2007) 'What Lies Ahead for Partnership Working? Collaborative Contexts and Policy Tensions?' *Journal of Integrated Care*, 15 (3): pp. 29–36
  This journal article provides an interesting exploration of joint working initiatives in England and Scotland.

- Petch, A. (2008a) *Health and Social Care: Establishing a Joint Future?* (Edinburgh: Dunedin Academic Press)

This short book provides a helpful and comprehensive account of the Scottish experience of joint working.

- Stewart, A., Petch, A. and Curtice, L. (2003) 'Towards Integrated Working across Health and Social Care in Scotland: From Maze to Matrix', *Journal of Interprofessional Care*, 17 (4): pp. 335–50

  This paper sets out the findings of research into the drivers and barriers to integrated care in a Scottish context.

Joint Strategic Needs Assessment

SEE ALSO **assessment; commissioning; joint commissioning; public health**

In addition to commissioning services in a more aligned way and developing more integrated service provision, health and social care have often been tasked with trying to understand jointly the needs of their local population. This has had a slightly different focus and ethos over time from the joint planning of the 1970s to the community care plans of the early 1990s. However, under section 116 of the Local Government and Involvement in Health Act, PCTs and local authorities are tasked with conducting an annual JSNA, defined by the Department of Health (2007b, p. 7) as follows:

> A systematic method for reviewing the health and wellbeing needs of a population, leading to agreed commissioning priorities that will improve the health and wellbeing outcomes and reduce inequalities.

Looking at both current and future needs over at least a 3–5-year period, JSNAs should inform the various strategic plans that each partner has to produce and should then be embedded in local *commissioning* intentions. While many local areas already had local processes for assessing population needs, this expertise and data often resided within the *public health* function and was not always seen as a whole systems responsibility. In addition, some mechanisms for assessing need were often *ad hoc* or only focused on one particular user group, with scope for JSNA to provide more of an over-arching vision of what is needed locally. As with all such processes, however, the trick has been to find ways of making JSNA an ongoing process and a live document, rather than a one-off annual technical exercise that sits on the shelf till we repeat the exercise in 12 months' time. Combining insights from our user *involvement* mechanisms with quantitative data from more traditional public health data sets has proved a challenge, with different underlying notions of what constitutes valid evidence in the first place. More recently, the duty to conduct an annual JSNA has also been boosted via the creation of a new public health function, based within local government and – in theory – bringing together the clinical and technical expertise of NHS public health experts with the broader health and well-being role of *local government* (see entry on *public health*).

Recommendations for policy and practice
- Irrespective of the quality of local relationships or the extent to which services are integrated or not, finding ways of jointly understanding the nature of the health and social care problems to be solved feels crucial.
- No matter how sophisticated the technical analysis presented in JSNAs, the key is making the JSNA a living document that is embedded in practice and genuinely informs the nature of joint endeavours.
- This involves drawing on the expertise of public health specialists, but mainstreaming these within the broader NHS/ local government and seeing public health as a resource for the broader system.
- In practice, health and social care have access to different types of data and tend to assess needs in different ways – and working with these cultural differences is probably just as important as the more technical aspects of JSNA.
- JSNA should not be a one-way process, telling commissioners and service providers what to do. Ideally, it will be a two-way process, where future JSNAs are also informed by the pressures commissioners/providers are facing and the questions they need resolving.

KEY TEXTS
- Ellins, J. and Glasby, J. (2008) *Implementing Joint Strategic Needs Assessment: Pitfalls, Possibilities and Progress* (Leeds: Integrated Care Network/Health Services Management Centre)

Early research study looking at the implementation of JSNA and exploring its potential to boost joint working.

A series of articles in the *British Medical Journal* offer a helpful series of insights into health needs assessment (and are typically free to access) – see Jordan et al. (1998), Stevens and Gillam (1998), Wilkinson and Murray (1998), Williams and Wright (1998) and Wright *et al.* (1998).

- Williams, I., Robinson, S. and Dickinson, H. (2011) *Rationing in Health Care: The Theory and Practice of Priority Setting* (Bristol: The Policy Press)

This moves beyond the subject of needs assessment to consider broader issues of decision-making and priority-setting once the needs assessment has taken place.

1

leadership

SEE ALSO culture; governance; trust; values

Over the last decade or so, leadership has become recognized as an increasingly important component in producing high-quality public services. There is no end to calls for 'better' and 'stronger' leadership on the assumption that this should lead to more effective outcomes for service users.

Often where accounts of unsuccessful attempts at inter-agency working are recorded, one of the reasons given for this is they lacked 'strong' leadership. In research from the United States, Kanter (1989) points to research indicating that while managers spend up to 50 per cent of their time initiating partnerships and a further 23 per cent of their time developing strategic partnership plans, they spend only 8 per cent of their time actually managing partnerships. Leadership and management seem to be considered important concepts then, but what do they mean?

Leadership is possibly one of the most researched topics of the past fifty years. Yet it remains a contested concept, under theorized and reliant on a few popular views and perspectives (Bolden and Gosling, 2006). The terms leadership and *management* are often used inter-changeably, although much of the literature proclaims that there is a clear distinction to be made. Where leaders are trans-formational, managers are transactional (Zaleznik, 1992). The former do the right thing, while the latter merely do the thing right (Bennis, 1994). Grint (2005) argues that the distinction between management and leadership is best understood through an analysis of the problem to be solved (wicked, tame or critical) and the nature of the *power* to be exercised (hard power or soft power):

- **Critical problems** require an immediate intervention with hard power and therefore demand a command response (where the priority is to provide an answer).

- **Tame problems** are the ones that organizations have seen before and thus have an established reaction – they require a managerial response (where the priority is to organize a process).
- **Wicked problems** are complex issues where we do not even understand the nature of the problem let alone the solution. These are often the sort of problems that health and social care partnerships are established to address and require a leadership response that deploys soft power (where the priority is to ask questions).

This is probably one of the more helpful frameworks to draw on when thinking about inter-agency leadership. In contrast to those who would make a firm distinction between leadership and management, Pye (2005) suggests that 'it seems much less significant when what really matters is (effective) organising' (p. 35). This suggests that we cannot think about leadership and management in isolation from the wider processes of *governance* and organizing.

There are many different definitions of leadership and often we find that these are closely linked to the types of *values, cultures* and social systems present within any kind of group. In practice, this means that groups expect different things of leaders and have different expectations of how power might be operationalized within any given setting. If groups hold different views on leadership, this can have important implications for inter-agency working. Yet, there is a relatively sparse amount of literature that directly considers leadership and management within inter-agency settings. In one rare account, O'Leary and colleagues (2006) define collaborative leadership as '[A] concept that describes the process of facilitating and operating in multiorganizational arrangements to solve problems that cannot be solved or easily solved by single organizations. Collaborative means co-labour, to cooperate to achieve common goals, working across boundaries in multisector relationships' (p. 7).

Some commentators (such as Kanter) have argued that the challenge of leading and managing in inter-agency settings is a more difficult task than operating in traditional *hierarchical* organizations. Inter-agency working may lack a common framework between partners; exhibit asymmetrical power relations (i.e. one partner holds more power than other(s)); possess incompatible values; have unclear authority and communication channels; and deploy different professional discourses. Echoing some of Kanter's themes, UK health and social care partnerships have tended to bring together organizations that are characterized by different *accountability* regimes, priorities, values, institutional rules, roles and rituals, diverse financial cycles etc. As such, some authors have suggested that leading and managing in inter-agency settings is fundamentally different to that of traditional organizations. Here the leadership and management of inter-agency settings is often equated to that of *networks*, which are thought to operate under the deployment of less 'hard' variants of power to those found in traditional (hierarchical) organizations. However, Peck and Dickinson (2008) warn against this oversimplification, arguing that the sorts of factors highlighted as different for inter-agency settings could also characterize individual organizations (e.g. fragmentation of responsibilities within agency boundaries and professional self-interest).

Recommendations for policy and practice

- There are many different definitions and understandings of leadership and management. It is important that when working with others you are clear about the definition you are working with.
- Different individuals and settings will value and legitimize different aspects of power and behaviours. Having an insight into these are key in understanding leadership across a range of different types of settings.
- Whether you require leadership or management responses in any particular setting depends on the types of problems that you are trying to address (e.g. critical, tame or wicked).
- It is argued that leadership and management of inter-agency settings are more challenging given a range of differences, yet this distinction is often in practice an over-simplification.

KEY TEXTS

- Grint, K. (2005) *Leadership: Limits and Possibilities* (Basingstoke: Palgrave Macmillan)

  This book provides a helpful account of the socially constructed nature of leadership.

- O'Leary, R., Gerard, C. and Bingham, L.B. (2006) 'Introduction to the Symposium on Collaborative Public Management', *Public Administration Review*, 66: pp. 6–9

  This is the introductory paper for a series of journal articles that directly deal with the issue of collaborative public management.

- Peck, E. and Dickinson, H. (2008) *Managing and Leading in Inter-agency Settings* (Bristol: The Policy Press)

  This accessible text provides an overview of the literature surrounding the management and leadership of inter-agency initiatives.

learning difficulties

SEE ALSO **co-production; mental health; personalization; safeguarding; social model**

There are an estimated 1.2 million people in England with learning difficulties, including nearly 300,000 children and some 900,000 adults (of whom 191,000 or 21 per cent are known to learning disability services; Emerson *et al.*, 2010). Although formal definitions vary, the Department of Health's previous *Valuing People* strategy (2001c, pp. 14–15) provides a helpful overview:

> Valuing People is based on the premise that people with learning disabilities are people first. We focus throughout on what people can do, with support where necessary, rather than on what they cannot do. Learning disability includes the presence of
> - a significantly reduced ability to understand new or complex information, to learn new skills (impaired intelligence), with;
> - a reduced ability to cope independently (impaired social functioning);
> - which started before adulthood, with a lasting effect on development.

> This definition encompasses people with a broad range of disabilities. The presence of a low intelligence quotient, for example an IQ below 70, is not, of itself, a sufficient reason for deciding whether an individual should be provided with additional health and social care support. An assessment of social functioning and communication skills should also be

taken into account when determining need. Many people with learning disabilities also have physical and/or sensory impairments. The definition covers adults with autism who also have learning disabilities, but not those with a higher level autistic spectrum disorder who may be of average or even above average intelligence – such as some people with Asperger's Syndrome.

Historically, services for people with learning difficulties were dominated by long-stay hospitals, with some people seen as 'incapable' of living a normal life in the community and placed in segregated institutional settings. In part this was felt to be for people's own protection and in part it may have been influenced by the eugenics movement (which attributed a range of social problems to inferior genes and was keen to ensure that people with learning difficulties did not reduce the future gene pool by 'being allowed' to 'breed'). In practice, some of the long-stay hospitals were anything but safe, and major scandals occurred in such isolated settings in the 1960s and 1970s. Nor were many people with learning difficulties 'incapable', and the more recent emphasis on concepts such as normalization and community care has led to significant deinstitutionalization, the closure of the long-stay hospitals and the development of a broader range of community-based services. This in turn has required greater inter-agency working – where the hospitals used to try to meet all people's needs (for health, housing, education, employment and so on), health and social now need to work together to support people to live independently (while also working with a broader range of universal services to help them become more accessible for people with learning difficulties).

Despite this need to work together, services for people with learning difficulties have often felt very divided – and the different professions tend even to use different language. While health tends to refer to *learning disability*, education talks about people with 'special educational needs' and social care tends to use the term 'people with learning difficulties'. Although all these terms can refer to slightly different groups with slightly different needs, a number of user-led organizations have anecdotally suggested that they prefer 'people with learning difficulties' as the best of a bad job – coining the slogan that 'labels are for jam jars not for people'.

They have also championed the phrase 'nothing about us without us' (now taken up by government as a key mantra for reform – albeit that government may mean something slightly different to the way in which this concept was originally developed). Services for people with learning difficulties were also the place where personal budgets were first developed in a meaningful way, and have thus been at the forefront of the *personalization* agenda.

In recent years, key developments within services for people with learning difficulties have included transferring funding from the NHS to *local government* (so that the latter is the lead commissioner), ongoing concerns about the welfare of people with learning difficulties who still live in NHS campuses or who are placed in independent hospitals, and the poor quality of care that people with learning difficulties can receive from some GPs and hospital wards (see Mencap, 2007; Michael, 2008). To try to respond to the latter, a model of 'health facilitation' has emerged, where specialist learning disability workers use their skills and knowledge not to care for people in segregated settings, but to support colleagues in general services to become more accessible for people with learning difficulties.

Recommendations for policy and practice
- Historically, services for people with learning difficulties show how integration by itself may not be enough – although services were integrated via the long-stay hospitals, this was not the right service model and a number of abuses occurred.
- Services for people with learning difficulties also show how different language and definitions of need can act as a barrier to more joined-up working.
- Rather than focusing on health and social care in their own right, policy documents such as *Valuing People* have tended to concentrate on trying to help people with learning difficulties live chosen lifestyles, with health and social care simply a means to a broader end of greater rights, choice, inclusion and independence. For some people, this might mean more integrated health and social care – but arguably other things such as family, friends, communities, housing, employment and leisure are more important.
- The concept of health facilitation deserves further consideration – rather than trying to integrate service structures,

they may be a scope to use models such as this to share skills and expertise more flexibly across current boundaries.

- Some of the most interesting developments in services for people with learning difficulties have come not from formal 'services' but from a broader inclusion movement (made up of people with learning difficulties, their families and key allies). This offers a very different view of how services can change, based more around notions of citizenship and rights than health and social care reform (see the entry on *personalization* for more discussion).

KEY TEXTS

- Duffy, S. (2003) *Keys to Citizenship: A Guide to Getting Good Support for People with Learning Disabilities* (Birkenhead: Paradigm)

  Practical guide as to how to focus services on helping people achieve citizenship.

- Mencap (2007) *Death by Indifference* (London: Mencap)

  Shocking accounts of what can go wrong when health services offer poor care to and discriminate against people with learning difficulties – see also Michael (2008).

- Williams, V. (2012) *Learning Disability Policy and Practice: Changing Lives?* (Basingstoke: Palgrave Macmillan)

  Health and social care textbook, exploring services for people with learning difficulties from a user-centred perspective.

learning disability

SEE **learning difficulties**

local government

SEE ALSO **accountability; area-based initiatives; Health and Well-Being Boards; social care**

While health care is organized nationally, both children's and adult's *social care* is run locally as part of a broader system of local government. Thus, these are services where practitioners and managers are accountable to locally elected politicians, funded in part by the local taxes people pay through their Council Tax. If people do not like the services they are getting or feel they are paying too much local tax, then they can vote for someone else at the next local election and, if enough people feel the same, change the nature of the administration. This is a very different kind of *accountability* to that which exists in the NHS, and the political nature of the system (with a small 'p' and sometimes with a capital 'P') can be very alien to NHS colleagues.

Local government is also funded in different ways to the NHS – with some of the former's money coming from the local Council Tax. Over time, the money available via central grants has been relatively fixed, with the only real revenue over which Councils have much control taking the form of Council Tax and charges for local services (both of which are often unpopular). This leads to a situation known as the 'gearing effect'. If a Council has a budget of £100 (to keep it simple), it might be made up of £80 from central fixed funds and £20 from local sources. If the Council wants to raise its budget to £105 to meet a new need or improve a service, this spending pressure falls entirely on the Council Tax/local charges. Thus, an increase of 5 per cent (£100–£105) leads to an increase in Council Tax/charges of 25 per cent (£20–£25) – which can look disastrous in the local media. This is entirely deliberate and is a way of the centre putting pressure on local areas to keep spending down. Under the Coalition government (2010–) local government has been promised greater flexibility in terms of how it manages and spends its money, although it is also facing substantial funding cuts and the suspicion remains that being given greater freedom over not enough money may not prove very liberating.

Another key difference is that social care is only a part of local government's remit (albeit a significant one). In addition to social care, other responsibilities can include functions such as education, roads, refuse collection and housing. To make things more complicated, some local councils are unitary authorities (i.e. they are responsible for most local services within one organization) while more rural Shire counties are typically two-tier authorities (i.e. they have an overall County Council responsible for some services and a series of district councils responsible for others).

Over time, the way that local government is organized has tended to evolve. In England, the *Every Child Matters* agenda saw the creation of a single Director for *Children's Services*, often bringing together children's social care with education. However, many areas found it difficult to integrate a universal service (education) with a service focused on specific groups of children (social care) and a number have now reorganized again. In some authorities a desire to reduce the number of senior posts is leading to new 'People' directorates (focusing on all services delivered to individuals, and separate from a 'Place' directorate). Politically, Councils are now overseen by a Council Leader and a cabinet (mirroring the structures of national government), with cross-party councillors sitting on 'scrutiny' committees (to scrutinize the work of the Cabinet – a little like Parliamentary select committees nationally). Although scrutiny initially focused on Council services, it has since been extended to include *health scrutiny* as a means of extending local government's role around health and well-being and introducing additional local accountability to the health service. Of course, whether this is a helpful assertion of the importance of local democracy or more of a token gesture depends on your point of view. In some areas, health scrutiny seems to have adopted an adversarial approach and the scope for genuine collaboration and improved accountability seems limited. Elsewhere, a more facilitative and joint approach has emerged, with a willingness to explore areas where the NHS and local government working together could add most value. The more recent advent of *Health and Well-Being Boards* may also help to develop a more locally accountable system.

Recommendations for policy and practice
- Having a locally led system has the potential to produce greater local accountability and a more responsive approach. However, having two different NHS and local government systems with different boundaries, funding mechanisms and systems of accountability can also make joint working harder.
- In practice, the complexity of local government funding can make it difficult for anyone to fully understand where any problems may lie. For example, if adult social care is facing significant cuts, is this because they have not done enough locally to protect this service? Have they consciously and legitimately decided to prioritize something else? Was the money they received enough in the first place? Are they being set up to fail by central government giving them responsibility

for something that cannot be delivered within current resources? Often the complexity of the system is such that it can be almost impossible for a non-expert to know – and even the experts might disagree.

- The ongoing reorganization of adult and children's services seems to prove the claim that 'your integration is my fragmentation' (Leutz, 1999). Rather than trying to change structures in order to improve joint working, perhaps the best way forward is to find ways of working across the boundaries wherever they happen to exist at any given time.

- While health scrutiny has the potential to improve accountability, there is a danger that committees adopt an adversarial 'select committee' approach and that this prevents the development of joint working, joint learning and mutual *trust*.

- Tensions between national and local government have always existed. Sometimes, central government finds it difficult to understand why approaches and outcomes seem to differ so much locally, and has to explore whether this is to do with genuine local differences or to do with poor performance (which can be quite difficult to tell from the centre). On other occasions, local government feels as if central government passes a lot of its own spending pressures onto local Council, leaving them to 'wield the axe'. There can also be concern about central pledges around increased spending – when you add all these up they are often claimed to come to more than the entire budget for that particular service area (a concept often described in terms of a 'Tardis effect').

KEY TEXTS

- Jackson, A. (ed.) (2011) *The Councillor's Guide, 2010–2011* (London: Local Government Group)

  Free online guide for new councillors providing an accessible introduction to the role, key structures and the main things new councillors need to know.

- Stoker, G. and Wilson, D. (2004) *British Local Government into the 21st Century* (Basingstoke: Palgrave Macmillan)

  Edited collection by leading authors.

- Wilson, D. and Game, C. (2006) *Local Government in the United Kingdom*. 4th edn (Basingstoke: Palgrave Macmillan)

  Key introductory textbook on local government, running to multiple editions.

long-term care

SEE ALSO **older people**

Historically, a range of long-term bed-based services for a number of community care user groups were provided in long-stay hospitals. However, from the 1960s and 1970s onwards, there was a growing reaction against this model of provision following a series of high-profile hospital scandals and with greater recognition that these *older people, people with learning difficulties* and *people with mental health problems* were not 'sick', did not need to be in hospital and could live more independent lives in the community. Over time, therefore, services that would once have been based in hospital were re-provided in the community, and support that would once have been the responsibility of the NHS has fallen under the remit of adult social care (see Means *et al.*, 2008; Glasby and Littlechild, 2004 for a summary). While many people would support this change philosophically, it also meant that long-stay services that were once free became the responsibility of means-tested social care (and hence that people began to pay – often very large amounts). At the same time, this shift in the health and social care divide caused significant confusion for local services and for patients/service users – with people unclear about their rights and responsibilities (and with significant local variation in interpretation). As Means and Smith (1998, p. 153) have suggested in their review of the community care reforms more generally:

> Such a situation was bound to encourage health authorities to run down their remaining nursing-home and continuing-care bed provision. Another certainty was that some local authorities would deny they had a responsibility for some people referred to them from acute hospitals, on the grounds that their needs were essentially those of health care and not social care. The boundaries of health and social care had shifted once more, with people previously perceived as ill now being increasingly defined

as having social care needs which are the responsibility of local authority and not the NHS ... This has emerged as one of the most significant features of the health and social care reforms of the 1990s.

Hardly surprisingly, this has generated a series of high-profile legal challenges and a number of attempts to develop clearer guidance and a more consistent system (see Department of Health 2009 for a summary of key issues and legal cases). There have also been a series of reviews of long-term care funding more generally – focused mainly not only on older people but also having implications for people of working age – in order to create a more equitable and transparent system (see, for example, Royal Commission on Long Term Care, 1999; Wanless, 2006; Dilnot, 2011). However, none of these have yet been implemented in full – with the exception of Scotland (where the Scottish government took a very different approach in response to the initial Royal Commission; see Bell and Bowes, 2006 for a review).

At the time of writing, people with long-term care needs are typically defined as being the responsibility of social care and are means-tested, while free NHS continuing health care is reserved for a small number of people who have particularly complex and severe needs. In practice, this seems to be defined in such a way that the vast majority of people seem to fall into the first rather than the second category, and a significant amount of time and energy still seems to be wasted deciding which person falls into which camp. As Department of Health (2009, pp. 4–7) guidance suggests:

'Continuing care' means care provided over an extended period of time, to a person aged 18 or over, to meet physical or mental health needs that have arisen as a result of disability, accident or illness. 'NHS continuing healthcare' means a package of continuing care that is arranged and funded solely by the NHS ... Deciding on the balance between LA and PCT responsibilities with respect to continuing care has been the subject of key court judgments.

Recommendations for policy and practice
• The funding of long-term care is highly controversial and very complex – and only a long-term political consensus can hope to offer enough clarity and stability to devise a solution.

- This is often portrayed as an economic issue (what we can afford) – but is actually a political issue (what we can afford really means what we are prepared to pay).
- The current approach to categorizing people and distinguishing between personal care, nursing care and continuing care seems indefensible and unworkable in practice (albeit that decisions are probably more consistent and transparent now than in the past).
- Often, these policy tensions play out for front-line staff, who find themselves having to work with service users who do not understand these technical distinctions and who feel angry, upset and let down. In this situation, staffs have to be the human face of a system they do not necessarily agree with.
- In an era of financial constraint, there is a risk that front-line professional relationships suffer and that patients are placed under undue stress as the tensions this system causes play out.
- Whatever happens next, the status quo seems increasingly unsustainable and something major probably has to give.

KEY TEXTS

- Bell, D. and Bowes, A. (2006) *Financial Care Models in Scotland and the UK: A Review of the Introduction of Free Personal Care for Older People in Scotland* (York: Joseph Rowntree Foundation)

  This reviews the experience of different parts of the United Kingdom in seeking solutions to the more general issue of long-term care funding.

- Department of Health (2009) *The National Framework for NHS Continuing Healthcare and NHS-funded Nursing Care,* July 2009 (revised)

  National guidance with details of key principles and legal cases.

  More general reviews of long-term care funding include the Royal Commission on Long Term Care (1999), the Wanless Review (2006) and the Dilnot Review (2011).

long-term conditions

SEE ALSO **acute care; community services; co-production; personalization; social model**

Although one of the key popular images of the NHS is of emergency care and of hospitals, the bulk of patients are people who have long-term conditions (also known as *chronic diseases*) that cannot be cured but that need ongoing management over time (such as diabetes, asthma, coronary heart disease and so on). According to the Department of Health (see www.dh.gov.uk/en/Healthcare/ Longtermconditions/tenthingsyouneedtoknow/index.htm for all statistics quoted in this paragraph), around 15 million people in England, or almost one in three of the population, have a long-term condition (including half of people aged over 60). People with long-term conditions account for 70 per cent of the primary and *acute care* budget in England (with around one-third of the population accounting for over two thirds of healthcare spend).

Hardly surprisingly, this has major implications for the way in which care is organized and delivered. Historically, services have been very focused around one-off, acute, episodic care. However, the bulk of people with long-term conditions need very different support, much more focused around self-care and around care provided in their own home and in the community.

In recognition of this, a series of policies have sought to shift care closer to home and to rebalance the system away from acute care towards more community-based approaches and support for greater self-management (see, for example, Department of Health, 2004, 2005, 2006a, 2006b). Drawing in particular on international models of chronic disease management and on high-profile US examples of good practice, key developments have included an Expert Patients Programme to support people to manage their own care, the advent of community matrons to support people with multiple and complex needs and a broader system of case management for people in between. While these are welcome developments, they have not yet proved enough to rebalance the system as a whole. Other areas of policy have also had the opposite effect, sometimes sucking more activity into hospitals (particularly the granting of *Foundation* status and the way in which acute hospitals are funded). Although the creation of community matron posts has added extra impetus, these workers have arguably been subjected to unrealistic expectations about their ability to create whole systems change and typically have high case loads that make it difficult to devote the amount of time that some patients might need. Despite a focus on 'expert patients', moreover, some health services have developed from very paternalistic origins, and the creation of more of a partnership of equals between the professional (who may have technical expertise) and the individual person (who is an expert in their own lives and what works for them) remains elusive. Perhaps just as fundamentally, the NHS has often been criticized for being a 'sickness' rather than a 'health service', and changing this historical orientation will take a substantial cultural shift.

Recommendations for policy and practice
- Focusing on long-term conditions is the right thing to be doing – but genuinely rebalancing the system away from its current and historical crisis focus will require sustained commitment and long-term cultural change.
- In the mean time, other policies (especially around hospital payment systems) can have unintended consequences and make this policy challenge even harder.
- At the heart of the long-term conditions agenda should be a recognition of the expertise of the person (who should be seen as an expert by experience with just as much to contribute to a potential solution as the NHS professional working with them).
- By sometimes badging this in terms of 'chronic disease management', policy has seemed to conceive of this primarily as a medical issue and may therefore have inadvertently limited the role of social care partners (who might not recognize this language and see that it also involves a change in practice for them too).
- Although we have identified 'community matrons' to try to keep people with complex long-term conditions healthy and out of hospital, there may be scope to explore the contribution of other groups (e.g. colleagues in social care or even practitioners from wider settings such as regeneration and community development) as well as peer support.

KEY TEXTS
- French, S. and Swain, J. (2011) *Working with Disabled People in Policy and Practice: A Social Model* (Basingstoke: Palgrave Macmillan)

  Inter-agency textbook focusing on disability and 'long-term conditions' but offering more of an alternative social model.

- Health Foundation (2011) *Helping People Help Themselves: A Review of the Evidence Considering Whether It Is Worthwhile to Support Self-Management* (London: Health Foundation)

Review of the underlying evidence base around self-care.

For a summary of international evidence and experience, see work by Chris Ham and Debbie Singh (Ham and Singh, 2006; Singh and Ham, 2005; Singh, 2006), Helen Parker (2009) and Powell Davies *et al.* (2009).

m

management

SEE leadership

markets

SEE ALSO commissioning; hierarchies; mixed economy of care; networks; New Public Management

Traditional organizational theory suggests that there are three primary ways that organizations interact with one another: through *hierarchies*, markets or *networks* (see the entry on *hierarchies* for an overview of each approach). A market approach is described as one where the transaction between two parties is mediated by a price mechanism. In a competitive market, this price mechanism should assure both parties that the exchange is equitable and this demand for equity attracts transaction costs. Because of their relatively high transaction costs, markets tend to encourage organizations to be fairly independent and only collaborate when necessary.

From the late 1970s, a series of national and international economic crises prompted the Conservative governments of Margaret Thatcher (1979–1990) to initiate a process of *market-based* reform. According to the ideology of these reforms, a very large public sector had become massively inefficient, consuming too much of the nation's resources, and serving the interests of staff and welfare professionals rather than people receiving services. In response, the Conservative government sought to reform public services according to market principles, with the public sector increasingly focused on purchasing services from a growing range of public, private and voluntary organizations, rather than providing them all 'in-house'.

Strongly influenced by NPM and its critique of hierarchies as large, unwieldy and inflexible, we have seen the separation of purchaser of services and providers in an attempt to produce markets in public services and therefore make these more effective. In theory, this is meant to keep costs down and encourage providers to be innovative and more flexible. Providers should compete for business that should make them even more cost effective and ensure that they deliver what service users want. Arguably, though, the degree to which markets have been able to be introduced within public services is more debated and in fact quasi-markets may be a better description for the resultant settlement. The concept of the quasi-market denotes the presence of some broadly market-based relationships but within a predominantly hierarchical setting (Le Grand and Bartlett, 1993).

Influenced by market type reforms, the dual agendas of choice and competition have taken hold in health and social care in recent years. In health care, patients have a choice of provider for elective treatments and providers are paid a fixed, centrally determined tariff for each procedure. The idea here being that providers will be incentivized to be innovative and more efficient in order to make a profit and be cheaper and better than other providers. This has also led to stimulation of the provider market with providers from beyond the public sector entering this field so that a *mixed economy of care* is produced. Social care has a somewhat longer experience of these sorts of mechanisms and there has been more of a mixed economy of care and greater self-funding and co-payment.

Recommendations for policy and practice
- There are three basic forms of mediating relationships between agencies – hierarchies, markets and networks.
- Many of the reforms introduced into the UK public sector from the mid-1980s onwards have been influenced by market-type reforms (e.g. choice and competition).
- It is argued that choice and competition should make providers of care more efficient and encourage them to provide more of what service user's desire.
- These agendas have also led to different types of organizations entering the health and social care field such as private providers and third sector organizations.
- In practice, true markets have not often been introduced in health and social care, and the system is more of a quasi-market.

KEY TEXTS

- Glasby, J. and Dickinson, H. (2008) *Partnership Working in Health and Social Care* (Bristol: The Policy Press)

  This text provides an overview of these concepts and applies them to an English health and social care context.

- Le Grand, J. (2007) *The Other Invisible Hand: Delivering Public Services through Choice and Competition* (Princeton (NJ): Princeton University Press)

  This text illustrates much of the type of thinking about the introduction of choice into public services.

- Sullivan, H. and Skelcher, C. (2002) *Working across Boundaries: Collaboration in Public Services* (Basingstoke: Palgrave Macmillan)

  This text provides a comprehensive introduction to the various theoretical underpinnings of collaboration.

medical model

SEE social model

mental health

SEE ALSO co-production; personalization; safeguarding; social model

In England, some 17.6 per cent of the population had at least one common mental disorder in 2007 (see Mental Health Network, 2011 for all key statistics in this entry), and it is often estimated that some one in four adults will seek help for a mental health problem at some stage of their life. For people with much more severe mental health problems, some 107,765 people received inpatient mental health care in 2009–2010 (a 5 per cent increase on the previous year). In prison, around 70 per cent of prisoners suffer from two or more mental disorders (compared to 5 per cent of men and 2 per cent of women in the general population). People with mental health problems are also much more likely than members of the general population to be unemployed (7.9 per cent of people in contact with secondary mental health services are in paid employment), are much less likely to be homeowners, are disproportionately represented among homeless people and suffer significant discrimination and stigma. Despite widespread media attention on high-profile mental health homicides, these are very rare and are even rarer when concerning an attack on someone not already known to the perpetrator. Most homicide is actually carried out by people without mental health problems, and the proportion committed by people with mental health problems has been decreasing during a period when more people with mental health problems are living in the community.

Over time, mental health has been a key area of inter-agency and inter-professional activity, recognizing that people rarely have clear cut needs that fall neatly into the remit of one organization or profession. This has included the formation of Community Mental Health Teams (often an informal grouping of local professionals coming together to provide care in a more multi-disciplinary manner) as well as more recent and more formal developments (such as Assertive Outreach, Crisis Resolution and Early Intervention teams – often referred to as 'functionalized' teams). Many areas have also used the *Health Act flexibilities* to create integrated mental health providers, formally merging their health and social services (see Peck *et al.*, 2002 for an innovative early example of this process). While the focus here is on relationships between health and social care, there is also a need to develop more primary care-based approaches and to make links between services for people with *long-term conditions* and for people with mental health problems (learning lessons from both physical and mental health settings).

Despite these developments, relationships between health and social care can also be difficult in mental health, with different professionals adhering to a range of underlying models relating to the nature and cause of mental ill health (including a series of biological/medical/psychiatric models and a series of more psychological and social approaches). Some social workers have also felt that their distinctive professional value base and contribution could be undermined by being merged into NHS-based 'Partnership' Trusts where health workers significantly outnumber social care staff (see Blinkhorn, 2004 for discussion of the role of social work in mental health services). Changes have also taken place to the traditional Approved Social Worker role to widen this to a broader range of professionals. Thus, of all the user groups reviewed in this book, mental health offers a fascinating case study and is something of an acid test – while joint working is as needed here as anywhere else and although there are significant opportunities, there are also a series of tensions and barriers to be overcome.

Recommendations for policy and practice

- Although mental health has often been seen as a separate and specialist services, there is much to be gained from approaches that can respond to physical and mental health needs in a more holistic manner (and there may be significant potential for developing links to services for people with long-term conditions).
- Joined up health and social care seems crucial in mental health – but just as important are links to and work around broader issues such as housing, employment and campaigns to reduce stigma and promote inclusion.
- The nature and causes of mental ill health remain contested, and more work is needed to support different disciplines to explore the implications of these potentially competing models.
- There is particular need to focus on the contribution and identity of social care staff who have been transferred to NHS settings, so that they are properly supported and feel confident enough to be able to work effectively with others from different backgrounds.
- Although other user group/patient settings sometimes look abroad for good practice examples, there is significant learning from Community Mental Health Teams and from 'Partnership' Trusts that could and should inform current debates.

KEY TEXTS

- Blinkhorn, M. (2004) *Social Worker: Leading Roles in Mental Health – Adjustment to Change, New Ways of Working and Other Potential Solutions* (Durham: Northern Centre for Mental Health)

  Interesting study of the role of the social worker in multi-disciplinary teams – see also, ADASS, 2008; Allen *et al.*, 2009; Tew, 2005 for discussions of more social approaches to and models of mental distress.

- Rogers, A. and Pilgrim, D. (2001) *Mental Health Policy in Britain.* 2nd edn (Basingstoke: Palgrave Macmillan)

  Leading mental health textbook, exploring the nature and history of mental health services as well as a series of policy and practice tensions.

- West, M. *et al.* (2012) *Effectiveness of Multi-Professional Team Working in Mental Health Care* (Birmingham: Aston University)

  National study into *teamworking* in adult mental health by Michael West and colleagues, leading researchers into the nature, quality and outcomes of teamworking.

mergers and acquisitions

SEE ALSO **area-based initiatives; Care Trusts; culture; Health Act flexibilities; Health and Social Care Trusts (Northern Ireland); hierarchies**

Mergers and acquisitions are important in the context of health and social care collaboration as many of the attempts introduced to forge closer working relationships between health and social care bodies have been structural in nature. The United Kingdom has seen a number of different structural entities introduced to bring about better inter-agency working practices through, for example, *Care Trusts*. However, frequent structural reform of the NHS (and to a lesser extent Local Authorities) has also caused difficulties in forging effective partnerships between health and social care, as frequent reorganizations can disrupt working relationships locally.

Mergers seem like they are a fairly simple concept and indeed McClenahan and Howard (1999, p. 4) describe a merger as 'the coming together into a single corporate body of two or more separate organisations.' However, Baskin *et al.* (2000) further differentiate mergers into three types:

- **Partition** – managers assume that things continue as they have with merged units operating side-by-side.
- **Domination** – one organization and its culture take over another.
- **Synthesis** – through careful planning, design and execution the merger brings out the best of both in order to create a super-ordinate harmony.

Each of these different types of mergers has different tensions and challenges. Partition may lead to tensions and conflicts arising from putting units together but not dealing with any of the practical challenges this poses. Domination may lead to resentment in the partner that has been taken over. Within the literature on health and social care partnerships, it has often been suggested that NHS partners dominate due to the size of their budget and power in relation to social care services. It is for this reason that commentators such as Hudson (2002a, 2002b, 2004) were critical of Care Trusts. Synthesis is the aim that underpins many collaborative endeavours in health and social care in an attempt that the 'sum be greater than the parts' (also described as 'creating collaborative advantage' – see Huxham and Vangen, 2005) – although achieving this in practice is challenging.

Acquisitions are probably closest to the domination model of mergers in practice. An acquisition involves acquiring control of another organization. This may be a horizontal acquisition where two similar organizations come together or a vertical acquisition where quite different types of organizations are brought together. Acquisitions may be uncontested where this arrangement is welcomed, but they may also be hostile where this course of action is not favoured by one of the parties involved. It could be argued that where organizations are of different sizes and relative *power* bases then all mergers are acquisitions (McClenahan and Howard, 1999). It might therefore be helpful to be explicit about the intentionality of any merger or acquisition processes from the outset to provide clarity and allay fears. Marks and Mirvis (2001) provide one framework that can be helpful in illustrating this (Figure 1).

Despite mergers and acquisitions being a staple tool of commercial and public sector organizations alike, the overwhelming message is that 'mergers, acquisitions and large organisational change rarely succeed in fulfilling the outcomes that they aim to achieve, and that assumed management cost savings are similarly rarely achieved' (Dickinson *et al.*, 2006, p. 4). It is suggested that 55–70 per cent fail to meet their anticipated purpose (Carleton, 1997) and an organization can expect a 25–50 per cent drop in productivity when going through large-scale change (Tetenbaum, 1999). The reason given most frequently to explain this failure is the 'human factor' (or *culture*). Essentially organizations are good at dealing with commercial and financial factors but pay less attention to the sorts of issues that impact on their staff in their everyday working lives and might cause stress to them. The literature is very clear that it is crucial to pay attention to the impact that these changes have on employees and to support them on an individual level.

FIGURE I   *Defining the integration end state*

Source: Adapted from Marks and Mirvis (2001, p. 85).

Recommendations for policy and practice

- UK health and social care organizations have been through a range of structural reforms over the last decade or so and these have caused difficulties in creating sustainable relationships and therefore collaborations between health and social care agencies.
- A merger is technically the coming together of two or more organizations, although the depth and the extent to which these organizations merge may have very different connotations for the organizations in practice.
- Much of the evidence suggests that large-scale organizational change is often ineffective and does not deliver the intended results.
- The most common reason for the failure of mergers and acquisitions is a failure to pay attention to the 'human factor' of change.
- Rather than focusing on creating new structures, it is crucial to consider the issue of culture.

KEY TEXTS
- Dickinson, H., Peck, E. and Smith, J. (2006) *Leadership in Organisational Transition – What Can We Learn from Research Evidence?*

Summary Report (Birmingham: Health Services Management Centre)

This research paper provides a summary of the literature on mergers and acquisitions and applies it specifically to a health care context.

- Edwards, N. (2010) *The Triumph of Hope over Experience: Lessons from the History of Reorganisation* (London: NHS Confederation)

  Accessible overview of lessons from NHS reorganizations – with a wonderful title.

- Marks, M.L. and Mirvis, P.H. (2001) 'Making Mergers and Acquisitions Work: Strategic and Psychological Preparation', *Academy of Management Executive*, 15: pp. 80–94

  This explores how to make mergers and acquisitions work – particularly how to pay attention to human factors.

method-led approaches

SEE **evaluation**

mixed economy of care

SEE ALSO **carers; commissioning; markets**

Although many people associate health care in particular with the public sector, welfare services in the United Kingdom have always been delivered by a mixed economy of care (i.e. by a mix of public, private, voluntary and informal provision). Rather than seeing health and social care as 'public services', therefore, it is more accurate to see them as funded and planned by public bodies – but potentially delivered by a wide range of organizations.

Over time, both New Labour and the Coalition have sought to increase competition and to *commission* services from a broader range of providers. However, this has been controversial – as a long but helpful quote from a former Chief Executive of the NHS suggests (Crisp, 2011, p. 91):

Most NHS staff and members of the public thought of the NHS in terms of the actual bricks and mortar of the hospitals and expected care to be given by NHS employed staff in NHS owned facilities. In the Department [of Health] however we were at this stage starting to think of the NHS as more like a guarantee or a promise of care. The NHS would make sure you were looked after well and got the care you needed whether you were treated in an NHS hospital or a charity or a private one. You would be an NHS patient in every case and entitled to the same standards, rights and privileges and you would access it in the same way through your GP, phone line or Accident and Emergency Department.

Thinking of the NHS in this way ... opened up enormous possibilities for innovative services. We were no longer bound by old restrictions as to who might offer a service or how ... Funding would continue to come from taxes and services would continue to be available to every citizen according to their need and regardless of their ability to pay. The NHS would continue to be free at the point of need but there would be greater flexibility in the way in which it was delivered.

Historically, many services that we now see as a key part of the welfare state were provided by voluntary organizations and by philanthropy, with people in need who could not access such support having to rely on the informal support of friends and neighbours and/or paying privately. Thus, the early forerunners of the social work profession, public housing, health visiting, ante-natal care, education for disabled children and old age pensions were all developed by voluntary organizations, eventually becoming so vital that they were taken on by the 1940s welfare state and became part of statutory provision. Those needing medical support often had to pay privately, and some groups of people banded together to jointly purchase support and spread the cost between members of the group (though friendly societies or mutual aid to cover the cost of medical care or of burial costs, for example).

After the Second World War, a range of services were provided by the state – but still with a role for a mixed economy of care. Thus, support provided by some six million unpaid family members, friends and neighbours is crucial to the lives of children and adults with health and social care needs. Voluntary organizations and private companies deliver a range of welfare services on behalf of the state, and the voluntary sector (sometimes known as the 'third sector') also has a key role in identifying new need and pioneering new forms of support. The hospice movement is also run on a charitable basis, and a range of patient groups look towards specialist charities for the in-depth knowledge and experience (e.g. around cancer, Alzheimer's Disease, MS, Parkinson's, etc). Some groups who see themselves as a key part of public services are also technically private – for example, GPs are often small-business people who sell their services back to the NHS (albeit that they would often see themselves and be perceived by the public as a core part of the NHS).

Although services are often broken down into four sectors (public, private, voluntary and informal), these categories overlap or blur around the edges. Thus, some voluntary organizations are often very small and informal – similar to the informal support provided by individual informal carers. Equally, some are large national or international organizations and often look much more like large private companies or public organizations. Some service users and family members have also set themselves up as small micro-enterprises, while models such as *social enterprise* can involve a mix of public, private and voluntary sector models and approaches. While this book focuses primarily on health and social care, this distinction is overly simplistic and masks a much more complicated reality.

Recommendations for policy and practice

- Although health and social care are often viewed as 'public services', it is important to be clear what we mean by this, as services have always been delivered by a mix of public, private, voluntary and informal sector provision.
- A key danger is that we say we value something about how each of these sectors delivers services – yet in the act of securing such services we make providers behave a little bit more like current services (thus gradually recreating the current system and losing what made them distinctive). This is a process known as isomorphism (see entry on *theory*).
- While some would claim that it does not matter who provides services (as long as they are good), others claim that the nature and value-base of providers *does* matter – and that we lose something important if the nature of provision changes dramatically.
- A key role is played by GPs, who they occupy an interesting space as one of the professions most trusted by the public

and a key foundation of the NHS, yet operating primarily as independent small businesses.

- Some approaches – such as social enterprise – blur traditional distinctions altogether. In principle, policy makers seem to be aspiring to an approach that can combine the best of public sector ethos, voluntary sector mission and private sector commercial acumen.

KEY TEXTS

While most health and social care textbooks focus (often implicitly) on public services, key sources for the other sectors include the following:

- Deakin, N. (2001) *In Search of Civil Society* (Basingstoke: Palgrave Macmillan)

  Review of civil society and voluntary action from a leading commentator on the role of the third sector.

- Drakeford, M. (1999) *Social Policy and Privatisation* (Harlow: Pearson)

  Critical review of the role of privatization in areas such as health, social security, housing and education.

- Kendall, J. (2003) *The Voluntary Sector: Comparative Perspectives in the UK* (London: Routledge)

  Detailed, research-informed and one of the leading UK textbooks on this topic.

- Work by Mike Nolan and colleagues (1996, 2003) on caring and family relationships.

multi-disciplinary working

SEE **partnership working**

n

networks

SEE ALSO **hierarchies; markets**

Traditional organizational theory suggests that there are three primary ways that organizations interact with one another: through *hierarchies*, markets or *networks* (see entry on *hierarchies* for explanation of these different forms). While markets and hierarchies have received much attention from organizational theorists and economists (see, for example, Weber, 1968; Arrow, 1974), work by sociologists and anthropologists (see, for example, Dore, 1973; Durkheim, 1933) suggested that these ideal types were insufficient in describing and explaining all contexts. These theorists recognized the power of cultural forces and observed that certain contexts encouraged the socialization of individuals into systems and under these circumstances individuals acted not according to the forces of price or the types of *power* associated with hierarchical relationships, but rather due to socio-cultural forces (institutions). These forms were therefore extended to include a further mode of 'the network'.

This third mode is characterized by actors recognizing complementary interests and developing inter-dependent relationships based on *trust*, loyalty and reciprocity to enable and maintain collaborative activity. It is proposed that within networks, actors are working towards the same aims and objectives and therefore generate trust. This reduces transaction costs and prevents the need for the same formal structures associated with hierarchies (although actors will likely be bound by shared understandings or informal rules).

More recently interest has grown in the concept of networks, which is often seen as a response to the implications of the changes of the 1980s and 1990s. The implication of market reforms was that public services had supposedly become increasingly fragmented, with a growing split between commissioners of services and providers from the public, private and voluntary sectors. This is described by Sullivan and Skelcher (2002, pp. 15–20) in terms of 'the hollowed out state', where government continued to be responsible for identifying what services were needed, but much less involved in actually delivering this. It was identified by the New Labour government that at the very time policy was starting to focus on more complex, cross-cutting social problems, the mechanisms for responding to this need were increasingly diverse and fragmented. Against this background, the response was a much greater emphasis on inter-agency working and partnership as a means of co-ordinating something of a patchwork quilt of services.

6 and colleagues (2006) undertook a systematic review of the literature on networks and guard against the assumption that all networks are the same. They identify a wide range of different types of networks, all of which are based on different types of connections through different actors and rely on a variety of resources to drive them. This work is important in the sense that it draws attention to the fact that networks can take many different forms and so we must be clear about which we are discussing or else risk misunderstanding.

Yet despite the notion of networks being widely embraced by academia, politicians and public sector professionals alike, Davies (2011) warns against assuming that either we have real networked *governance* in practice or that this should lead to the types of outcomes promised in the literature: 'contemporary governance has little in common with the visionary regulative ideal of networks. Rather, "networked" governance institutions look very like the "modernist" hierarchies they were supposed to replace' (p. 3). Davies adds to some of the more critical voices who suggest that networks do not always deliver positive outcomes and, as others such as O'Toole and Meier (2004) illustrate, there are potential negatives to networks.

Recommendations for policy and practice
- There are three ideal forms of mediating relationships between agencies – hierarchies, markets and networks.
- Many of the reforms introduced into public services from the mid-1990s onwards were heavily (rhetorically at least) influenced by the notion of networks.

- Networks are seen to be a helpful mode of governance as they are based on horizontal, trust-based relationships, which are flexible and have the capacity for innovation.
- However, there are a range of different types of networks and so we need to be careful in thinking about the type of network we are discussing and the relative merits and support mechanisms that this requires.
- We cannot assume that we will always get the positive outcomes associated with networks and there is also the potential for negative implications to flow from this mode of interaction.

KEY TEXTS

- 6, P. *et al.* (2006) *Managing Networks of Twenty-First Century Organisations* (Basingstoke: Palgrave Macmillan)

  This book provides a comprehensive review of the literature on networks.

- Davies, J. (2011) *Challenging Governance Theory: From Networks to Hegemony* (Bristol: The Policy Press)

  This book provides a detailed account of the critiques of the place of networks within contemporary academic theory.

- Sullivan, H. and Skelcher, C. (2002) *Working across Boundaries: Collaboration in Public Services* (Basingstoke: Palgrave Macmillan)

  This text provides a good introduction to the various theoretical underpinnings of collaboration.

New Public Management

SEE ALSO **governance; markets**

NPM is a management paradigm that emerged from the late 1970s onwards and gained international attention. NPM varies from country to country in its implementation and commentators such as Ferlie *et al.* (1996) have suggested that it is not *one* paradigm, but a cluster of several. What these paradigms share, though, is a belief that big government is an unhelpful way of organizing the design and delivery of public services. NPM is critical of bureaucracy, suggesting that it is an inflexible way of organizing that has a tendency to be too hierarchical. *Hierarchies* are often associated with top-down decision-making process, which are thought to be too distant from the expectations of citizens and *service users*.

In critiquing the public sector, NPM drew on the commercial sector for its recent experiences. In the United Kingdom, from the 1980s onwards due to deregulation, many commercial sector organizations became exposed to large-scale national and international competition. Those who succeeded in this environment were those who became more efficient and also offered consumers the types of products that they wanted. NPM theorists argued that while the commercial sector had undergone radical change the public sector remained 'rigid and bureaucratic, expensive, and inefficient' (Pierre and Peters, 2000, p. 5). NPM has therefore sometimes been seen as an attempt to apply private sector management techniques to the public sector.

Different advocates of NPM vary in their descriptions of this approach, but Peck and Dickinson (2008) distil this concept into the following characteristics – NPM:

- emphasizes establishment and measurement of objectives and outcomes;
- disaggregates traditional bureaucratic organizations and decentralizes management authority;
- introduces *market* and quasi-market mechanisms;
- strives for customer-oriented services.

Another important strand of this type of approach is that with the decentralization of *power* to a local level and a focus on customer (or service user) outcomes, what is important for public services is that they 'steer, not row'. The implication here is that if governments concentrate more on *what* should be delivered (and performance manage this), instead of *how* it should be delivered, then they will be more effective.

But what is the relevance of this management paradigm to inter-agency health and social care? Arguably many of the major reforms of health and social care over the last twenty-five years can trace their roots back, at least in part, to ideas derived from NPM, from the introduction of general management in the NHS and compulsory competitive tendering (CCT) of local authority goods and services in the 1980s, through the purchaser–provider splits of the

1990s, to the plurality and choice agenda of the twenty-first century. NPM-type principles are also at the heart of many of the reform processes that have taken place in relation to the *commissioning* agenda in health and social care and so it has had a fundamental impact on the institutional arrangements and broader context we find ourselves with today.

In addition to the system-wide implications of this philosophy, there are also important implications in terms of the ways that public sector organizations are managed and led. Old public administration was often described as being inward looking and run in the interests of the professional staff who work within public services, not in the interest of service users (Harrison *et al.*, 1992). NPM brought with it a focus on 'new managerialism' where individual managers were *accountable* for the success or otherwise of organizational objectives. Since NPM began to take hold within the United Kingdom we have seen greater emphasis on the role of *leadership* and management roles within public sector organizations.

Recommendations for policy and practice
- NPM is a broad philosophy that suggests that overly bureaucratic and hierarchical ways of organizing are inefficient and often ineffective. This philosophy suggests that public service organizations should focus more on outcomes and what service users want, rather than the actual delivery of these services (steering not rowing).
- NPM has been a driver for many of the health and social care reforms that have taken place in the United Kingdom over the last 30 years, particularly in terms of the separation of purchaser and payer functions.
- At an organizational level, NPM has led to a greater focus on outcomes and performance management, and has led to different types of leadership and management roles with individuals, not organizations, taking more responsibility for organizational objectives.

KEY TEXTS
- Ferlie, E. *et al.* (1996) *The New Public Management in Action* (Oxford: Oxford University Press)

  This text provides a helpful overview of the concept of NPM, particularly within the context of the United Kingdom.

- Peck, E. and Dickinson, H. (2008) *Managing and Leading in Inter-Agency Settings* (Bristol: The Policy Press)

  This book provides an overview of the phenomenon of NPM and draws out the implications of this type of approach for English health and social care.

NHS Commissioning Board (NHS England)

SEE ALSO **Clinical Commissioning Groups; commissioning**

When Gordon Brown was about to become Prime Minister after Tony Blair stepped down, rumours circulated that he would look to do something dramatic in a number of different policy areas in his 'first 100 days' in charge. Within health care, an idea that seemed to be seriously being considered was to delegate greater responsibility for the NHS to an 'independent board', much more arms-length from government (thus, removing the NHS from day-to-day political interference). As commentators at the time suggested (Glasby *et al.*, 2007, p. 2):

> While Nye Bevan said that the sound of a dropped bedpan in Tredegar should reverberate around the Palace of Westminster, he surely would not have wanted to distribute bedpans, empty them and clean them out all by himself.

This was similar to ideas being debated by the then Conservative opposition, and also built on a series of previous discussions around similar issues (see, for example, Dewar, 2003). As Sir Alan Langlands (2003, p. 18), former NHS Chief Executive, observed:

> Political interest in the NHS ... is more intense than ever ... There has been no serious debate for some time about the pros and cons of distancing the NHS from direct political control ... There must be a way of maintaining proper public accountability whilst liberating the system for overtly political interventions and knee-jerk reactions.

In practice, the Coalition government has introduced a 'National Commissioning Board' or *NHS Commissioning Board* (NCB), with the then Chief Executive of the NHS in England becoming the first Chief Executive of the new NCB. When this organization took up its new powers in April 2013 it chose the name 'NHS England'. According to the Department of Health (NHS, 2011, p. 3):

> The Government has set out a clear vision for a modernized NHS driven by a new commissioning system focused relentlessly on improving outcomes for patients. The cornerstone of the proposed system will be local clinical commissioning groups, which will put GPs – using their knowledge and understanding of patients' needs – at the heart of the commissioning process.

> Clinical commissioning groups will be supported across the country by clinical networks, bringing together experts on particular conditions and service areas, and by clinical senates, bringing together a range of clinical voices across particular parts of the country.

> At national level, the new NHS Commissioning Board will ensure the new architecture is fit for purpose and provides clear national standards and accountability – it will put the 'N' in NHS. The Board will lead the delivery of improvements against the NHS Outcomes Framework and of more choice and control for patients.

Based in Leeds, the NCB has 27 local Area Teams and is nationally accountable for the outcomes achieved by the NHS. It has responsibility for a budget of some £95 billion (of which nearly £65 billion is allocated to CCGs). It also holds contracts for local *primary care* and dental services, as well as commissioning a range of specialist services. A key mechanism is an annual 'mandate' – a statement of what the NHS is meant to achieve that allows the Secretary of State to hold the NCB to account. Further details are available via http: // www.commissioningboard.nhs.uk/ (including publicly available videos of Board meetings).

Recommendations for policy and practice
• Initial debates about an 'independent' Board seem to have given way to talk of a 'national' Board, and it remains to be seen how arms-length from government such an entity can really be in practice.
• In the process, there needs to be a balance struck between appropriate political accountability for significant public money

and day-to-day freedom from excessive political interference in the running of the service.

- One way of doing this may be for the government to set the overall budget and the outcomes to be achieved – but for NHS England to decide the most appropriate structure and service delivery mechanisms to deliver these.
- In practice suspicions remain that NHS England will not necessarily feel or behave significantly differently to previous structures and leadership teams.
- A key early challenge will be to ensure enough local flexibility for the new CCGs, while still keeping a tight grip of NHS finances – and this may prove a difficult balance to strike.

KEY TEXTS

- Dewar, S. (2003) *Government and the NHS – Time for a New Relationship?* (London: King's Fund)

  This explores the case for an 'NHS Agency' separate from government.

- Glasby, J. *et al.* (2007) *'Things Can Only Get Better?' – the Argument for NHS Independence* (Birmingham: Health Services Management Centre)

  Policy paper exploring initial debates about NHS 'independence' and possible models.

- NHS (2011) *Developing the NHS Commissioning Board* (London: NHS)

  NHS document setting out early thinking around the nature and development of the NCB.

O

older people

SEE ALSO co-production; hospital discharge; intermediate care; long-term care; personalization; safeguarding; social model

In the United Kingdom, a series of technological and demographic changes has meant a significant increase in the numbers of people aged 65 and above (and a particular increase in the number of people aged 85 and above– sometimes referred to as 'the oldest old'). As the government has suggested (HM Government, 2009, p. 38):

> By 2026, population estimates show there will be double the number of people aged over 85 that there are now, and the number of people aged over 100 will quadruple ... We can see these changes in our own families:
> - A girl born in 1920 could expect to live to around 60.
> - Her daughter born in 1950 could expect to live to around 70.
> - Her granddaughter born in 1980 could expect to live to her mid-70s.
> - Her great-granddaughter born in 2008 could expect to live to her early 80s.

While this is sometimes described in the media and in popular conversation as a 'burden', it is actually a major achievement of medical technology and the welfare state. Because of the progress we have made, there are many people alive today who would previously have died – and this should be cause for celebration. Of course, such changes do increase pressure on a range of services (particularly health and social care), but this seems a fantastic problem to have and not something which we should allow to be portrayed as a 'burden'.

Typically, adult social care has separated its work into services for older people, for *disabled people* and for people with *learning difficulties* and/or *mental health* problems. However, the NHS does not conceptualize its work in the same way. Although the bulk of people using NHS services are older people, they are not seen as a discrete user group in their own right. Given that older people are the biggest users of the NHS, all health services are effectively older people's services. At the same time, joint working is made even more complicated by the fact that mental health services for older people can often be provided by specialist mental health Trusts separately from physical health services (while adult social care tends to work with frail older people and people with dementia together as part of its older people's directorate).

As with *long-term conditions*, a part of the problem is that many health care services have been designed to focus on people with a one-off crisis who need acute care – not necessarily people with a series of ongoing, fluctuating conditions. Thus, hospital services can treat someone if they have an immediate crisis in their health, but the person may well have a series of ongoing needs that require input from either community health or social care (and often both). Thus, the needs of frail older people or of people with dementia can often fall somewhere in between the remits of current agencies – everybody's priority and nobody's priority at the same time. Over time, this has been particularly evident in areas such as *hospital discharge, intermediate care* and *long-term care*, and the experience of older people can often be a god test of the quality (or otherwise) of local relationships.

Above all, a key priority has been how best to invest in prevention and rehabilitation to help people remain independent as long as possible and to regain as much independence as possible after any bout of ill health or hospital admission. While everyone now recognizes that denying people support until they reach crisis is counterproductive, it remains challenging to rebalance the current system (see Allen and Glasby, 2010 for further discussion). In particular, key issues include the lack of a clear evidence base, the long-term timescales required to embed prevention (which are often different to political timescales), the subsequent tendency to focus on short-term pilot projects and the need to focus on people with more severe needs. This can also be exacerbated by some of the tensions created by the funding mechanisms used in *acute care* and echoes many of the challenges facing the *long-term conditions agenda*. Overall, health and social may need to work together more effectively to respond to an ageing population – but creating a genuinely preventative system remains elusive.

Recommendations for policy and practice

- The growing number of older people is a major achievement and should never be seen as a 'burden' – indeed, it's hard to think of anything more offensive (as the implication is presumably that we would rather fewer older people were still alive).
- Having said this, demographic and other changes are placing greater strain on services that were not designed with current demography and society in mind. Although many people feel that major reform is required, there is little sign of the political consensus that might be needed to produce a sustainable, long-term solution.
- A particular fault line lies around the funding of long-term care, and solving this seems a long way off. Although policy debates often focus on different mechanisms for funding services, a more productive way forward may be to begin more of a national debate about the kind of older people's services we want and how much we're collectively prepared to pay for this.
- Although the NHS in particular does not break down its work in this way, older people are the biggest user group of health and social care. In this sense, most issues facing health and social care are actually older people's issues (even if we do not always conceive of them as such). While this makes joint working even more important, it can also make it even harder (as it affects so many different parts of the system at once).
- Older people with multiple and often fluctuating long-term conditions may need a particularly joined-up response from health and social services, and can often be something of an acid test of the quality of local relationships.

KEY TEXTS

- For an overview of the nature and development of community care services for older people and other adult user groups, see key texts by Means *et al.* (2008), Glasby (2012b), McDonald (2006) and Lymberry (2005).

- Key reviews of long-term care funding have been conducted by the Royal Commission on Long-term Care (1999), Sir Derek Wanless (2006), HM Government (2009) and Andrew Dilnot (2011).
- Mandelstam, M. (2008) *Community Care Practice and the Law.* 4th edn (London: Jessica Kingsley)

  Regularly updated, very accessible but detailed overview of the legal framework, key test cases and some of the major tensions.

optimist approaches

SEE theory

outcomes

SEE evaluation

outputs

SEE evaluation

p

partnership working

SEE ALSO culture; evaluation; inter-professional education; networks; teamworking; theory

Whenever the issue of inter-agency collaboration is debated, the first sticking point is always language. Even reading the other entries in this book so far (see, for example, the entry on *teamworking* for one set of definitions), it will be clear that there is a wide range of terms, often used imprecisely and inter-changeably (and with different authors using the same terms to mean slightly different things). To cite but a few examples, different accounts talk about concepts such as collaboration, inter-agency working, integration, inter-disciplinary working, inter-professional working, multi-disciplinary working, seamless care, strategic collaboration, transdisciplinary working, whole systems working and so on. Indeed, Leathard (1994, p. 5) alone identifies 52 different terms, describing this as a 'terminological quagmire'. While most authors comment on this 'definitional chaos' (Ling, 2000, p. 83), they can sometimes make it worse by reviewing previous definitions and then coming up with their own. Rather than add to this complexity, the current entry seeks to draw out key themes in the broader partnership literature and signpost below to further sources.

First and foremost, many of the definitions imply a spectrum of activity and relationships, ranging from fairly loose, informal co-ordination of efforts to much more long-term, formal, structured and/or large-scale initiatives. For Leutz (1999), for example, the key approaches are around 'linkage' (helping people with simple needs access other local services as appropriate), 'co-ordination' (more explicit processes or structures to address particular points of tension or discontinuity) and integration (creation of new, unified structures or processes for people with complex or unpredictable needs). For Curry and Ham (2010), a helpful distinction can be drawn between work at 'micro' (co-ordinated care for individual service users), 'meso' (where providers seek to deliver integrated care for a particular care group or populations with the same disease or conditions, through the redesign of care pathways and other approaches) and 'macro' level (where providers deliver integrated care for whole populations). This has similarities to Glasby's (2003) work on hospital discharge, which distinguishes between individual, organizational and structural approaches. For Glasby and Peck, moreover, there are a range of options around 'depth' (extent of formal integration) and 'breadth' (range of partners), with no one perfect organizational structure, but with different projects with different aims needing to work with partners in different ways to achieve desired outcomes (see, for example, Glasby, 2005).

Second, many definitions identify key characteristics – a sense of added value that partners on their own could not achieve, a sense of sharing rewards and risks, a relationship that is voluntary where individual partners can exit if they wish to at any stage, and a relationship that is long-term and ongoing. Sometimes, the latter can be seen in terms of a journey (Glasby and Dickinson, 2008), where we might not yet know our ultimate destination but recognize that we must travel at least part of the way together.

Above all, many accounts focus on the experience of service users and patients, arguing that something should only be classed as integrated or delivered in partnership if it feels that way to people on the receiving end. This seems a key measure of success, although, in our experience, many of the partnerships that have been evaluated at local level struggle to demonstrate improved outcomes for individual service users and often point instead to more efficient and effective organizational processes. While these might be expected to improve outcomes for individuals in the longer term, it seems harder to prove better outcomes in practice (see the entry on *evaluations* for a more detailed discussion).

Irrespective of the structures within which people work, it is ultimately what happens at ground level between different health and social care practitioners that matters for service users and patients. Thus, many discussions of partnership working can focus on organizational and policy issues, but sometimes neglect the issue of collaboration in frontline practice. Of course, it's here that the very real needs of service users and the constraints of the broader system combine – with practitioners often having to do the best they can for the people they are trying to support in difficult circumstances and with structures that were not necessarily designed to reflect the complexity of people's lives. While there are few easy answers, part of the solution may lie in individual practitioners trying to do their best to get to know and understand other professionals, investing time in building relationships, trying to see the situation from other people's point of view, treating other people as they would like to be treated themselves and always looking for ways of building their own knowledge and skills.

Recommendations for policy and practice

- Although it is often used imprecisely, the concept of 'partnership' nonetheless seems important – and intuitively there must be situations where there is a scope for the 'whole to be greater than the sum of its parts' (to use an everyday phrase).
- Although different definitions of 'partnership' may seem a largely semantic and academic issue, it remains important that people or organisations trying to work together are clear about what they mean by different terms and that they all understand the same thing about what they are trying to do and why.
- Key to this is the issue of outcomes – it depends what you are trying to achieve and for whom as to who you need to work with and how.
- In the past, 'partnership' sometimes seemed an automatic policy response (without sufficient clarity about what was trying to be achieved and why working with others in particular ways was the best way of doing this). This has sometimes been emphasized by asking: if partnership is the answer, what was the question?
- Whatever happens to future policy and structure, it is the way in which individuals in front-line practice work together (or not) that can make the most difference to service users.

KEY TEXTS

- Glasby, J. and Dickinson, H. (2008) *Partnership Working in Health and Social Care* (Bristol: The Policy Press)

  Short, pocket size, introductory textbook designed to review key theory, concepts, policy and practice.

- Glendinning, C., Powell, M. and Rummery, K. (eds) (2002)
  Partnerships, New Labour and the Governance of Welfare (Bristol: The
  Policy Press)
  Helpful edited overview exploring the partnership agenda under New
  Labour.

- Leathard, A. (ed.) (2003) *Interprofessional Collaboration: From Policy to
  Practice in Health and Social Care* (Hove: Routledge)
  Multi-disciplinary textbook exploring health and social care
  collaboration in terms of key concepts, policy, practice and
  interprofessional learning.

patients

SEE **co-production; personalization**

personalization

SEE ALSO **co-production; involvement; power**

From the late 2000s onwards, adult social care reforms have
increasingly been described in terms of a personalization agenda.
Summarized in the government's *Putting People First* concordat
(HM Government, 2007, p. 2), this agenda was clear that:

> Ensuring older people, people with chronic conditions, disabled
> people and people with mental health problems have the best
> possible quality of life and the equality of independent living
> is fundamental to a socially just society. For many, social care
> is the support which helps to make this a reality and may
> either be the only non-family intervention or one element of
> a wider support package. The time has now come to build on
> best practice and replace paternalistic, reactive care of variable
> quality with a mainstream system focussed on prevention, early
> intervention, enablement, and high quality personally tailored
> services. In the future, we want people to have maximum choice,
> control and power over the support services they receive.

In many ways, this seemed similar to broader notions of *co-production*
(Needham and Carr, 2009) and built on previous attempts to
involve people in decisions about their own care and to harness the

expertise by experience of people using services. While social care tends to talk about *service users* and the NHS about *patients*, this agenda was arguably more about seeing people as citizens with an entitlement to certain levels of support and to the same degree of choice and control over their services and hence over their lives as anyone else.

When talking about personalization, the government has tended to mean a series of different approaches to public service reform, which include better advice and information, an emphasis on developing greater social capital, a more preventative agenda and greater choice and control for people using formal services. Of all these, it is the latter that has proved not only the most exciting but also the most controversial, with policy and practice focusing on two linked but slightly separate approaches (see Glasby and Littlechild, 2009 for a summary):

- **Direct payments**: invented by groups of disabled people and implemented formally in 1996 following a sustained campaign by disabled people's organizations, this involves giving individual service users the cash equivalent of the directly provided services they would have received. While people can use this to hire a voluntary or private agency, they can also hire their own personal assistants and become employers in their own right. Experience to date suggests that practical and peer support from disabled people's Centres for Independent Living (CILs) is particularly important.
- **Personal budgets**: developed from 2003 by a national social innovation network known as 'In Control' (and sometimes referred to as a system of 'self-directed support'), personal budgets involve being clear with the person from the outset how much money is available to spend on meeting their needs and giving them greater choice over how this money is spent on their behalf. In theory, the personal budget can be spent in any way that legitimately meets the person's assessed needs, and can take a number of forms (a direct payment to the individual, a sum managed by a third party who knows the person well and cares about them, or a notional budget that the system manages on people's behalf).

From the beginning, both approaches seem to have had extremely positive effects, with service users reporting greater satisfaction, a greater sense of choice and control, greater continuity, fewer unmet needs, greater use of community rather than institutional forms of provision and a series of positive changes in many aspects of their lives. Moreover, all this seems to have been achieved for either the same – or possibly slightly less – money. In a challenging financial context, this raises an exciting possibility that we may be able to use scarce public resources more efficiently by ensuring that decisions that really matter to people are taken as close to the person they effect as possible (ideally by the person themselves or at least by someone near them who knows them well and cares about them) (see Glasby and Littlechild, 2009; Glendinning *et al.*, 2008 for a review of the research evidence to date).

Although beginning in adult social care, both direct payments and personal budgets have spread to other sectors (see, for example, Alakeson, 2007, 2011 for discussions about personal health budgets). However, from the beginning, these ways of working have tended to divide opinion, with some seeing them as two of the most funda-mental reforms of the welfare state in its history and some concerned that this may represent a form of privatization by the backdoor and an attempt to undermine public service values and ethos (see Glasby and Littlechild, 2009 for a more detailed discussion).

In terms of inter-agency collaboration, there are two main impli-cations. First of all, adult social care has adopted this way of working wholesale – and all adult social care in future will be delivered by personal budgets (except in an emergency). This means that any NHS workers will have to be familiar with the concept of person-alization if they are to work effectively with social care colleagues. Secondly (and more fundamentally), previous attempts to promote joint working have often tried to join services up top-down (via management structures, budgets and so on). In contrast, the person-alization agenda suggests that people may be able to join their own services up in a way that makes sense to them, ensuring integra-tion bottom-up. Perhaps if the current system could find a way of pursing greater integration top-down and bottom-up, while also enabling these approaches to meet in the middle, then we would see very significant and profound change indeed.

Recommendations for policy and practice
- For some commentators, the advent of direct payments and personal budgets are two of the most important and exciting developments since the initial creation of the welfare state in the 1940s.
- Although the personalization agenda began and is most well established in adult social care, it has spread to health and to children's services, and could have broader implications for housing, social security, education, community development and the tax and benefit system.
- Although personal budgets are often seen as a form of privatization by the back door, they are actually about citizenship and about changing the nature of the relationship between the state and the individual.
- In theory, being clear upfront about how much money is available to spend can be liberating for both service user and the worker – increasing scope for innovation and for responses more fully tailored to people's individual needs and circumstances.
- However, a key risk is that we make personalization more complicated than it needs to be, and that we gradually allow the old system to recreate itself under the guise of the new language. If this happened, it would be the worst of all worlds – promising rhetoric that only serves to set service users and workers up to fail.

KEY TEXTS
- Glasby, J. and Littlechild, R. (2009) *Direct Payments and Personal Budgets: Putting Personalisation into Practice.* 2nd edn (Bristol: The Policy Press)

  First major UK textbook exploring the nature, emergence and impact of direct payments and personal budgets.

- Glendinning, C. *et al.* (2008) *Evaluation of the Individual Budgets Pilot Programme* (York: Social Policy Research Unit)

  Official Department of Health-funded evaluation of personal budgets.

- Needham, C. (2011) *Personalising Public Services: Understanding the Personalisation Narrative* (Bristol: The Policy Press)

  Key study of the spread of personalization across different areas of the welfare state.

pessimist approaches

SEE **theory**

physical disability

SEE ALSO **co-production; long-term conditions; personalization; safeguarding; social model**

One of the key user groups for local authorities is people of working age with physical disabilities. Although some Councils organize their services as part of more generic community care teams (e.g. bringing together physical disability and services for *older people*), many have separate teams specializing in support for people of working age. In the NHS, the approach is different again, with policy and practice increasingly focusing on people with *long-term conditions* (who are often older people, although this also includes people of working age).

Whatever the structure locally, focusing on the needs of disabled people is crucial. According to government analysis, there are around 11 million disabled adults (one in five of the population), with social security spending for disabled people of nearly £30 billion and over two-and-a-half million people claiming incapacity-related benefits (see Prime Minister's Strategy Unit, 2005 for all data in this paragraph). Faced with widespread discrimination and with services that all too often deny people sufficient choice and control over their lives, disabled people can face a series of difficulties in terms of employment, income, housing and accessing community resources and facilities. In response, the previous New Labour government committed to a more rights-based approach to disabled people, promising that 'by 2025, disabled people in Britain should have full opportunities and choices to improve their quality of life, and will be respected and included as equal members of society' (p. 53). This is an important but bold pledge – and fundamental social, economic and cultural changes may be needed if it is to be achieved.

Central to services for disabled people is the notion of a *social model* of disability and the concept of independent living. Although disabled people are often portrayed as dependent on others, the reality is that we are all interdependent to a greater or lesser extent.

Thus, 'independent living' does not mean doing everything for ourselves, but – in keeping with the 2005 commitment – simply refers to the need for disabled people to have the same choice and control over their lives as non-disabled people.

Over time, some of the major changes that have taken place in health and social care have been led not by services or professionals – but by disabled people and their organizations. Often, this has adopted a more citizenship-based approach, reforming services through a civil rights campaign rather than through incremental changes in service provision. Thus, disabled people and their organizations have campaigned for legislation to promote greater rights and equality and for access to direct payments (see the entry on the *personalization* agenda). They have also developed user-led organizations such as Centres for Independent Living, and have been central in defining and promoting a social model of disability as an alternative to traditional medical models. For health and social care agencies trying to work together, these concepts offer a radical way of thinking about integration (see French and Swain, 2011 for more detailed discussion). Rather than welfare professionals trying to join up systems, services and bureaucracies, disabled people have articulated a vision based around citizenship and equal rights where formal services are seen as allies to support disabled people to live chosen lives. While inter-agency collaboration would undoubtedly flow from this, it would simply be a means to a much broader end rather than an end in itself.

Recommendations for policy and practice
- As with other user groups, health and social care have an important role to play – but living a good life depends just as much on a range of other things (such as strong communities, family and friends, employment, an adequate income and so on).
- Achieving these might not only require changes to health and social care, but also need a series of more fundamental reforms based around citizenship, civil rights and independent living.
- These are exciting, but potentially very new concepts to some professions and disciplines, and in-depth work is needed to explore our own *value* bases and the *outcomes* we are jointly trying to achieve.

- Current structures can make it difficult to join up social care 'physical disability teams' with the NHS long-term conditions agenda.
- Key advances have come from disabled people themselves as they have rejected traditional approaches and definitions and developed their own alternatives.

KEY TEXTS

- French, S. and Swain, J. (2011) *Working with Disabled People in Policy and Practice: A Social Model* (Basingstoke: Palgrave Macmillan)

  Focusing specifically on health and social care, this textbook adopts a social model to develop more integrated approaches.

- Prime Minister's Strategy Unit (2005) *Improving the Life Chances of Disabled People* (London: Prime Minister's Strategy Unit)

  Although dated and not fully enacted, this strategy document adopts a broadly social model and offers a very different, more citizenship-focused approach to future welfare reform.

- For further discussion of medical and social models, key contributions are by disabled academics and campaigners such as Michael Oliver (1990, 2009; Oliver and Barnes, 1998; Oliver and Sapey, 2006).

pooled budgets

SEE Health Act flexibilities

power

SEE ALSO accountability; co-production; governance; hierarchies; involvement

The issue of power is a prominent one within studies of organizations and the inter-agency literature is no exception to this rule. Many accounts of inter-agency working allude to the notion that differential power relations have posed difficulties in collaborative working practices in a number of different ways. However, any attempt to debate these issues first requires an understanding of the concept of power itself (and this has been understood in different ways).

The first – and probably most familiar – definition of power understands it a sort of resource (where an agency or individual can be said to have more power than another). In this respect, there are a range of potential sources of power including information; expertise; credibility; stature and prestige; uncertainty; access to top-level managers and the control of money, sanctions and rewards; and control over resources (Clegg *et al.*, 2005). If these are some of the potential sources of power, we also need to think about the different ways in which power might be exercised. Lukes (1974) suggests that power can be exercised in three ways:

- **Direct decision-making:** A has power over B, so that A can get B to act in such a way and do something that B might not otherwise do (e.g. through contractual requirements).
- **Non-decision making:** A prevents the issues or questions that are in B's interests, but not in A's, from surfacing (e.g. through excluding items from the remit of the partnership board).
- **Defining interests:** A may exercise power over B 'by influencing, shaping or determining his very wants' (e.g. through framing a problem in a particular way) (Lukes, 1974, p. 23).

The first two ways of exercising power are likely to be more familiar to us than the final one, which is perhaps a slightly different way of thinking about power given that it involves trying to influence and shape the way that other partners think about problems and solutions to issues. These first two are essentially a 'zero-sum' game in the sense that an actor has power or they do not. These different ways of exercising power also more readily lend themselves to some organizational contexts than others. For example, as we indicate above, the first way of exercising power can be linked to contracts and therefore *market* forms of organizing, while 'direct decision-making' and 'non-decision making' are often linked to *hierarchical* forms of organizing. These may be perceived as quite negative ways of operationalizing power in the sense that they may appear coercive, as though an individual or actor is forcing another into action.

The final way of exercising power seems less coercive in the sense that it is not directing others into action and is a more subtle means of deploying power. This way of viewing power is not as a resource, but instead as a property of relations and interactions between individuals and/or agencies. This means of exercising power has been more associated with *network* forms of organizing. The key implication of this is that we should be more interested in how power is manifest in practice. Clegg (1989) argues that in thinking about power the social and systematic elements that form the context in which individual interactions occur are important. The significant point here is that social and systemic aspects provide a framework within which action takes place. Not only are there many forms of power structures that surround our action and that might constrain the agency we have to act within any particular situation, but there are also a range of resources that we might draw on to facilitate the exercise of power.

When working in inter-agency settings, we are typically bringing together agencies with distinct ways of organizing. Different ways of organizing bring with them different concepts of what or who might be classed as authority, what *accountability* looks like and how power is conceptualized, legitimized and manifested (Peck and Dickinson, 2008). For example, in bringing together an NHS Trust and a Local Authority Social Services Department to work collaboratively, there are different notions of power given that the NHS is accountable centrally, whereas Local Authorities answer to their local populations via local elections. Each of these different partners will have professionals within their organizations who have different status and degrees of power and control. These are but a few simple examples of the different types of ways that power might manifest itself in relations and there are potentially many more. In bringing these partners together in an effective collaboration then allowing for both ways of organizing to exist may be crucial. Over-exerting the particular concepts of power and legitimacy for one partner could alienate the others and therefore lead to conflict or resistance to actions or activities (Peck *et al.*, 2004 provide an example of this happening within a health and social care setting).

Recommendations for policy and practice
- There are a range of different sources of power and at least three ways of exercising power. In thinking about any given context, it is helpful to reflect on the types of power that are available to you and your partners and therefore what the most effective ways of interacting might be.
- Power is not simply a resource but also resides in the relations between individuals. This means that coercion or power over

individuals are not the only sources of power and working to shape the values of a partner may be as, if not more, effective than attempts to directly apply power.

• Privileging one form of power over others may serve to alienate partners, particularly if they tend to work with different notions of power.

KEY TEXTS

• Lukes, S. (1974) *Power: A Radical View* (Basingstoke: Palgrave Macmillan)

This book provides an overview of the key definitions and debates surrounding the notion of power.

• Peck, E. and 6, P. (2006) *Beyond Delivery: Policy Implementation as Sense-Making and Settlement* (Basingstoke: Palgrave Macmillan)

This book provides some worked examples of where different concepts of power and organizing have come into conflict with one another. While most are set within a health setting, one explicitly deals with an example of a joint commissioning board.

• Peck, E. and Dickinson, H. (2008) *Managing and Leading in Inter-agency Settings* (Bristol: The Policy Press)

This text provides an overview of the notion of power and its applications in the leadership of inter-agency settings.

primary care

SEE ALSO **acute care; Clinical Commissioning Groups; commissioning; community services; Health and Well-Being Boards; NHS Commissioning Board; social care**

While there is considerable local variation, the primary care team usually consists of a range of different workers, including GPs, practice nurses, district nurses, health visitors, practice managers, administrative staff and, potentially, a series of attached staff (such as nurse practitioners, community psychiatric nurses, physiotherapists, counsellors and so on). Although this includes a number of different disciplines and professions, a lead role has often been played by GPs (whose origins as a profession date back many hundreds of years). Ironically, although GPs are seen as the lynch pin of a crucial public service, they have typically been private businesses, operating like a small legal or accountancy firm and selling their services to the NHS. When the health service was first created in 1948, GPs fought hard to retain their independent status, and they continue to operate on a different contractual basis to other health and social care professions (with relatively little policy makers or managers can do to influence their behaviour except for incentivizing them – often financially).

Given that the vast majority of the population are registered with a GP and that GPs are one of the most trusted professions by the general public, primary care is a crucial, low stigma, locally based arena from which to deliver services. In financial terms, moreover, entry to other parts of the health service often begins with a referral from a GP, and so the services provided and the decisions made in primary care can has a significant impact on the cost of health care and levels of usage of hospital and specialist services. For these reasons, there have been a series of attempts over time to give GPs and primary care greater incentives to provide additional services locally and thus reduce hospital admissions. The latest version of this in England – the advent of CCGs – is an attempt to give GPs control over significant NHS resources in order to reduce pressure on spending. Whether this is a good way of controlling costs or runs the risk of turning GPs into rationers of care rather than champions of the individual patient probably depends on your point of view.

Initially, many GP practices were small-scale, often single-handed practices – sometimes even run out of the front room of the GP's house with their partner as the receptionist and/or practice manager. Over time, however, primary care has become much more professionalized and specialist, with services increasingly provided by much larger practices out of purpose-built facilities and with a series of previously hospital-based services transferring into the community. In principle, the architects of the clinical commissioning reforms hope that this will accelerate this process, creating larger consortia of GPs that begin to share good practice, develop joint systems and provide a more high-quality, standardized service. Whether this is what people want or what GPs will feel comfortable providing (and whether something important about the relationship between GP and patient will be lost in the process) remains to be seen.

Recommendations for policy and practice

- The United Kingdom has a well-developed system of primary care – and this is a crucial resource from which to reform health services more generally.
- Engaging GPs and giving them greater financial incentives to develop community-based alternatives to acute care is crucial if the system is to rebalanced.
- However, primary care has often centred on the relationship between the GP and the individual patient – and becoming responsible for the health of whole populations may change the nature of this encounter.
- GPs are often independent contractors or small-business people, and there is scope to harness their entrepreneurial skills for the system as a whole. However, there is a danger that in order to do this, policy makes GPs behave more like the PCTs that they have replaced and that something important about their contribution is lost.
- Genuine clinical engagement is likely to depend on having the ability to influence what happens locally. If a new system becomes even more centralized than the previous one, then the very GPs policy makers have sought to involve could be alienated from the reform process.

KEY TEXTS

- Peckham, S. and Exworthy, M. (2003) *Primary Care in the UK* (Basingstoke: Palgrave Macmillan)

  Overview of the development of UK primary care since the 1980s.

- Rummery, K. and Glendinning, C. (2000) *Primary Care and Social Services* (Abingdon: Radcliffe Medical Press)

  Research-based guide to joint working between social and primary care, set against the backdrop of key changes in primary care in the late 1990s.

- Smith, J. and Goodwin, N. (2006) *Towards Managed Primary Care: The Role and Experience of Primary Care Organizations* (Aldershot: Ashgate)

  Detailed research-based review of the development of primary care organizations in England.

private sector

SEE mixed economy of care

public health

SEE ALSO commissioning; Joint Strategic Needs Assessment; local government

In a classic quote, public health was defined by C.E. Winslow (1920, p. 23, quoted in Baggott, 2010, p. 4) as:

> The science and art of preventing disease, prolonging life and promoting physical health and efficiency through organized community efforts for the sanitation of the environment, the control of communicable infections, the education of the individual principles of personal hygiene, the organization of medical and nursing services for the early diagnosis and preventative treatment of disease, and the development of social machinery which will ensure to every individual in the community a standard of living adequate for the maintenance or improvement of health.

Initially, public health was a responsibility of *local government* and was overseen by the Medical Officer for Health (see Gorsky, 2007 for an overview of this role). However, public health transferred across to the NHS in 1974 as part of a broader reorganization of services, albeit that many Directors of Public Health (DPHs) are often *joint appointments* between the NHS and local government (see Hunter, 2008 for further discussion of these roles). In 2010, the Coalition government's *Healthy Lives, Healthy People* public health strategy (HM Government, 2010b) set out an intention to create 'a new public health system in England to protect and improve the public's health, improving the health of the poorest, fastest' (p. 52). Among a number of proposals was a lead responsibility for local government, with a ring-fenced budget and DPHs transferring to upper-tier and unitary local authorities:

> Embedding public health within local government will make it easier to create tailored local solutions in order to meet varying local needs. It will also enable joint approaches to be taken with

other areas of local government's work (such as housing, the environment, transport, planning, children's services, social care, environmental health and leisure) and with key partners (such as the NHS, the police, business, early years services, schools and voluntary organisations) ... We will keep to a minimum the constraints as to how local government decides to fulfil its public health role and spend its new budget. (p. 53)

As the new system develops, it seems as though local government will take the lead for 'improving health and co-ordinating local efforts to protect the public's health and wellbeing, and ensuring health services effectively promote population health' (Department of Health, 2011b, p. 1). A new national body, Public Health England, will go live from 1st April 2013, taking a lead around a national health protection service, supporting the specialist public health workforce and proving information and intelligence to support local services.

While these changes have the potential to create a more joined-up approach to health and well-being, there are also concerns that this may dilute the clinical expertise of public health clinicians, that current terms and conditions may be adversely affected by local authority salary scales and that some local Councils may not prioritize public health to the same extent as the current system. The role of Director of Public Health will also presumably shift from being a high profile champion of public health to more of an advisor to elected members – with a series of subsequent *cultural* challenges.

Recommendations for policy and practice
- Of all the disciplines covered in this book, public health is one of the most significant areas where a multi-agency, whole system approach is required. Almost by definition, no public health expert or department can hope to be successful in isolation, and some form of partnership is essential.
- Over time, public health responsibilities have shifted between local government and the NHS. However, whatever the structure at any given time there is scope for significant added value from bringing together the technical and clinical expertise of public health with the broader well-being agenda of local government.
- Although adult social care has often been a key point of contact for the NHS, it is crucial that public health can link to the full

range of local authority services and departments (including housing, planning, economic development and so on).

- As public health shifts back to local government (in England), there is a risk that *structural change* causes initial upheavals. However, the longer-term challenges may well be cultural as DPH and other staff change roles and seek to become embedded in a local government setting.
- Whatever happens, massive health inequalities are a key issue for the NHS and local government alike – and it is difficult to overstate the size of the challenge.

KEY TEXTS

- Baggott, R. (2010) *Public Health: Policy and Politics*. 2nd edn (Basingstoke: Palgrave Macmillan)

  One of the leading introductory textbooks on public health.

- Berridge, V. (1999) *Health and Society in Britain Since 1939* (Cambridge: Cambridge University Press)

  Short but detailed review of health policy, health and society since 1939 from a leading public health historian.

- Hunter, D.J. (2003) *Public Health Policy* (Cambridge: Polity)

  Hunter, D.J., Marks, L. and Smith, K.E. (2010) *The Public Health System in England* (Bristol: The Policy Press)

  Key textbooks by a leading commentator and researcher on health systems and public health. David Hunter is also the lead on a national study of public health partnerships (Hunter *et al.*, 2011).

public sector

SEE **mixed economy of care**

q

quasi-markets

SEE markets

r

realist approaches

SEE theory

regulation and inspection

SEE ALSO accountability; governance; mixed economy of care

One of the challenges often traditionally cited in respect to inter-agency working is that of the processes of regulation and inspection (Glendinning *et al.*, 2005). At an organizational level, these are essentially the processes by which we can be sure that health and social care providers are conforming with appropriate standards and delivering care in the appropriate way (and this is the focus of this entry). Of course, individual health and social care professions also have to register with the relevant professional regulator (such as the General Medical Council for doctors) – and this can cause additional friction if individual professional bodies require their practitioners to practise in slightly different ways, have different approaches to continuing professional development and/or have slightly different professional codes of conduct. However, the way in which individuals practise is also influenced by the broader organizational context and the wider system within which they work – and the regulators of health and social care services have a key role to play in helping to shape this.

Until recently, health and social care organizations had different regulators and this caused difficulties for joint working as partners were subject to different regulatory frameworks. Prior to 2009, the regulation of health care (in England) was carried out by the Healthcare Commission, while social care was regulated by the Commission for Social Care Inspection. Following the Health and Social Care Act of 2008, the Care Quality Commission (CQC) was established to replace these two bodies and also the Mental Health Act Commission (which regulated mental health services). The CQC acts as a single integrated regulator for health and adult social care meaning that these services do not any longer need to be inspected and regulated by separate bodies.

There are different approaches in other parts of the United Kingdom, with Northern Ireland also having an integrated health and social care regulatory body in the form of the Regulation and Quality Improvement Authority (RQIA). In Wales, health- and social care inspection are still separate with the Healthcare Inspectorate Wales (HIW) agency responsible for health care services and the Care and Social Services Inspectorate Wales (CSSIW) overseeing the inspection and review of local authority social services. This is a similar scenario to Scotland where the newly formed Healthcare Improvement Scotland has been designed to support health care providers to deliver high-quality, evidence-based, safe, effective and person-centred care and to scrutinize services to provide public assurance about the quality and safety of care. Healthcare Improvement Scotland works alongside the Care Inspectorate, which is responsible for the regulation, inspection and support of improvement work around care, social work and child protection.

Prior to the establishment of the CQC, integrated services in England might find themselves being bound by two separate regulatory and inspection processes, which could not only create additional workloads but also on occasion lead to services trying to work to contradictory agendas. However, the newly merged CQC has since had high-profile problems of its own – and has been the subject of significant press speculation and negative media coverage (see Department of Health, 2012 for a review). On one reading, perhaps it is possible for agencies to be too large and too integrated, being tasked with serving too many different audiences and responsible for too many different functions at once.

Recommendations for policy and practice
- Until recently, health and social care services were often regulated and inspected separately, which caused some problems for partners who would inevitably end up working to different agendas.
- These difficulties were felt to be most pronounced in integrated services where professionals might be asked to work to two different regulatory schemes.

- While an integrated regulator may seem like a positive step forward, the new CQC in England has had a chequered history to date.
- In the longer run, perhaps an approach based more on the delivery of shared outcomes might be more fruitful (see the separate entry on *evaluation*).

KEY TEXTS

- Department of Health (2012) *Performance and Capability Review: Care Quality Commission* (London: Department of Health) (official review of the CQC)
- Social Services Inspectorate (SSI)/Audit Commission (2004) *Old Virtues, New Virtues: An Overview of the Changes in Social Care Services over the Seven Years of Joint Reviews in England, 1996–2003* (London: SSI/Audit Commission)

  Interesting summary of lessons learned from seven years of reviews conducted jointly by the former SSI and the Audit Commission.

risk

SEE **safeguarding**

S

safeguarding

SEE ALSO children and young people; learning difficulties; mental health; older people; personalization; physical disability

Safeguarding essentially involves protecting a particular group from abuse and neglect and ensuring that they receive safe and effective care. We probably most often encounter safeguarding in the context of *children's services*, although this is equally applicable to adult and *older people's services* and are important wherever we have vulnerable individuals and groups. Safeguarding is more than simply the protection of an individual from abuse; it is about the well-being and socio-economic inclusiveness of these individuals. In recent years we have seen a large degree of policy and practice interest in the field of safeguarding since the passing of the Human Rights Act (1998) and a series of high-profile abuse cases in both adult and children's services.

In children's services, the language of safeguarding has been around since the Children Act 1989, but arguably came to the forefront of policy under the New Labour government who made a number of pledges in terms of child poverty and social exclusion. These notions of safeguarding are broader than those that we had previously embraced, going beyond simply that of child protection. With the death of Victoria Climbié and the publication of *Every Child Matters* (Department for Education and Skills, 2003), the well-being agenda for children was expanded and it was acknowledged that joint working between a range of agencies would be necessary in order to achieve this.

In adult's services, the language has shifted somewhat away from speaking about 'vulnerable' adults and *adult protection* to *safeguarding* in recognition that this involves more than simply protection and involves a desire to support individuals to retain independence, well-being and choice. This broader definition still incorporates a right to live a life free from abuse and neglect, but is more than a narrow focus on these issues (ADASS, 2005). Although it is recognized that inter-agency working is essential in safeguarding adults, often specific teams have been established with a mandate around this function. While this offers a clear focus on safeguarding, such an approach has been criticized as it means that is seen as a 'minority concern of specialist individuals and teams' (Petch, 2008b, p. 30) and not at the heart of all services.

Although there has been a lot of attention paid to safeguarding in recent years, there is a question over the degree to which this activity is judged to be effective. Broadhurst *et al.* (2009) are critical of the approach adopted in the safeguarding of children over the last decade or so, arguing that although the rhetoric is about well-being, active citizenship and inclusivity, in practice a punitive approach to welfare delivery has emerged for those unable to 'play by the rules'. Services have become preoccupied with identifying, assessing and intervening on the basis of *risk*, which can individualize the social problems of children. Paradoxically the wealth of policy making in this area and the roll out of various initiatives intended to encourage more joined up solutions for children may actually have served to further fragment services.

In adult services, the attention to the concept of safeguarding is slightly more recent but again there is little in the way of evidence that this agenda has had a positive impact in a widespread way. Petch (2008b) suggests that safeguarding is bedevilled by a number of issues such as communication and *information sharing* where there can be concerns over what should be kept confidential and what information might be shared. It is important to set out local communication processes at a range of levels (individual, organizational and external) so that professionals are clear about what information can be shared. Differences in organizational *cultures* and *values* can also pose challenges for agencies trying to work together and investing time in understanding these can also facilitate better joint working.

More recently, the *personalization* agenda has also raised different questions about safeguarding. Manthorpe *et al.* (2010) have researched this emerging agenda with a view to establishing whether the aims of personalization and safeguarding are developing together as a coherent agenda or if they are being developed alongside but separate from one another. The research team concludes that adult safeguarding co-ordinators are not as engaged with other areas of social care as they might be and that their intelligence and experiences were not regularly accessed. This is surmised to be a missed opportunity to help address some of the tensions raised through personalization and points to the importance of linking safeguarding expertise with other areas of practice.

Recommendations for policy and practice
- Safeguarding is a broad concept that goes beyond just thinking about the protection of individuals and incorporates a range of aspects relating to well-being and inclusion.
- Safeguarding should be a core concern of public services and be a key priority for all, rather than simply just a concern of specific teams.
- Major difficulties that can emerge in relation to safeguarding relate to a clash of cultures and values and to communication difficulties. Having conversations about these issues in advance may forge more effective joint working.

KEY TEXTS
- Association of Directors of Social Services (2005) *Safeguarding Adults: A National Framework of Standards for Good Practice and Outcomes* (London: ADASS)

  This report sets out a best practice guide for safeguarding in the context of adult services.

- Broadhurst, K., Grover, C. and Jamieson, J. (2009) *Critical Perspectives on Safeguarding Children* (Oxford: Wiley)

  This edited collection provides a critical and evidence-based review of child safeguarding policy and practice.

- Petch, A. (2008b) 'Safety Matters: The Role of Partnership Working in Safeguarding Adults', *Journal of Integrated Care*, 16 (6): pp. 29–40

  This journal article provides a summary of the issues relating to joint working and safeguarding in the context of adult services.

seamless care

SEE **partnership working**

Section 75 agreements

SEE **Health Act flexibilities**

service users

SEE **co-production and personalization**

social care

SEE ALSO **commissioning; local government; mixed economy of care; personalization; safeguarding**

Although social care lacks an official definition, its key roles are often to provide practical support with activities of daily living for people who cannot do these tasks for themselves and to protect and promote the well-being of children and young people. As the Social Work Taskforce (2009, p. 5) states:

> When people are made vulnerable – by poverty, bereavement, addiction, isolation, mental distress, disability, neglect, abuse, or other circumstances – what happens next matters hugely. If outcomes are poor, if dependency becomes ingrained or harm goes unchecked, individuals, families, communities and the economy can pay a heavy price. Good social workers can and do make a huge difference in these difficult situations.

Historically, services have been tended to be organized via generic Social Services Departments based within *local government*. These were created in the early 1970s and were designed to bring together practitioners specializing in work with particular client groups, producing greater scope to work with whole families and whole communities. While the main profession is that of social work, the broader social care workforce includes a wide range of qualified and unqualified roles, ranging from home care assistants and day centre officers to social workers and to Directors of Social Services (who were often qualified social workers by background until relatively recently). Although the NHS has often enjoyed high-profile public support, social care is a less well-understood service and has historically lacked the same policy focus and status as health services.

Following the NHS and Community Care reforms of 1990–1993, adult social workers were increasingly badged as 'care managers' who would no longer work with people over the long term, but who were now responsible for *assessing* needs and designing 'care packages' to meet these needs from a *mixed economy* of public, private and voluntary services. Adult social care also became responsible for arranging and funding residential and nursing care (the cost of which had sometimes been borne by the national social security system). Over time this has meant that services have come under increasing financial pressure as the population has aged, and some of the current funding crisis is almost certainly the result of this 1990 decision to transfer responsibility for a rapidly escalating national budget for local government to resolve. Despite these changes, the underlying legal framework for adult care has traditionally been very patchy, based on a series of statutes from the 1940s onwards and arguably no longer fit for purpose (see, for example, Law Commission, 2011).

In children's services, the 1989 Children Act provided a more coherent overarching framework for children's social care. However, the pressures in children's service have been immense, with the need to focus on children at most risk of serious harm often feeling as if it has reduced scope to support children and families with lower level needs before a major crisis occurs. Over time, a series of high-profile child protection scandals and a number of very visible inter-agency failings have also had a serious impact on morale and the ability to recruit and retain staff. Despite a number of high-profile reviews (see, for example, Laming, 2003, 2009; Social Work Taskforce, 2009), children's services all too often suffer from negative and critical media coverage, poor public understanding and a deep-seated ambivalence within broader society as to whether the task is to care for people in need or to act as an agent of state controlling the behaviour of families where children are at risk.

In England, adult and children's services were separated following the Laming review of 2003, leading to the creation of new Directors of Children's Services (bringing together children's social care and education) and new Directors of Adult Social Services (often taking responsibility for other functions too such as housing, leisure and/ or the relationship with the local NHS). The same split has not occurred in other parts of the United Kingdom, and some English authorities are now reversing their earlier decision to break up children and adult services (see the entry on *local government*).

Recommendations for policy and practice
- Social care is a crucial service for many adults and children, yet has often been low status, poorly understood and the subject of significant ambivalence from the public and policy makers alike.
- This contrast strongly with the popularity and high profile of the NHS, and such differences in status can make joint working harder.
- Social care is based within local government (which is overseen by locally elected councillors and which can raise some of its own funding through Council Tax and user charges). Arguably, this gives social care a different kind of relationship to local people than is the case in health care, and these different forms of *accountability* can again cause inter-agency tension.
- Although services for children and adults have increasingly diverged (in England), generic Social Services Departments were created to produce a more holistic response to complex family and community needs. In a worst-case scenario, we could create increasingly inter-agency services for children and for adults, but make the gap between the two even greater.
- Although many Directors of Social Services were once qualified social workers by background, current Directors come from a range of disciplines and do not necessarily have direct experience of front-line practice. While these broader skills and experience can be invaluable, there is a risk that professional *leadership* and expertise is reduced if there is too great disconnect between senior leaders and the front-line.

KEY TEXTS
- For adult social care, the Law Commission's (2011) report on *Adult social care* provides a detailed review of adult social care legislation with widespread proposals for future reform (see Secretary of State for Health, 2012 for a government response). For children's services, two national reviews by Lord Laming (2003, 2009) provide a critical analysis of current provision and a stock-take of recent progress and ongoing problems.

- Key textbooks by Malcom Payne (2005a, 2005b, 2006) review the origins of social work, the nature of professional social work and the key theories that underpin social work practice.
- Skills for Care (2010) *The State of the Adult Social Care Workforce in England, 2010* (London: Skills for Care)

  Overview of the social care workforce with key statistics and quantitative data.

social enterprise

SEE ALSO **community services; mixed economy of care**

Social enterprise is a type of organization that is defined not by its need to create profit but by its ethos and social aims. Social enterprises are broadly defined as 'business[es] with primarily social objectives whose surpluses are principally reinvested for that purpose in the business or in the community, rather than being driven by the need to maximise profit for shareholders and owners' (Department of Trade and Industry, 2002, p. 13). A social enterprise is, first and foremost, a business that is engaged in some form of trading, but this trade is primarily to support a social purpose. Social enterprises are like businesses in that they aim to generate surpluses, but unlike private businesses, these surpluses are then re-invested into the local community or the social problem that the organization was set up to address.

Social enterprise is not a new concept by any means and its origins date to the co-operative movement of the nineteenth century or even friendly societies that date back to the seventeenth century (Marks and Hunter, 2007). Social enterprise is also an international concept, which has distinct roots in different nations (Teasdale, 2009). Social enterprise gained renewed attention under the New Labour governments (1997–2010) as part of their wider attempts to stimulate third sector involvement in the delivery of welfare services. From the mid-2000s onwards, we have seen considerable interest in this organizational form and its role in health and social care. Although difficult to count precisely, it is estimated that over 6000 social enterprises are involved in delivering health and social care services in the NHS (Social Enterprise Coalition, 2009).

Elsewhere in this book, we talk about the influence of *NPM* and its critique of *hierarchical* modes of organizing. These concepts are also important in terms of thinking about the recent renewed interest in the concept of social enterprise. Essentially traditional public sector organizations (hierarchies) are seen as being inflexible in terms of the needs of service users, inefficient and also not managing to engage professionals actively as they are employed to perform particular functional roles and not ultimately to go beyond this in ensuring the success of that organization. This means that these professionals do not necessarily have a personal interest in making a success of the organization, but in doing their own specific job well. Of course this incentive is present in commercial organizations, but some people are nervous of private sector involvement in the delivery of health and social care as this may be seen as companies gaining profit that could be spent on important public services (Pollock, 2005).

In principle, some believe that social enterprise offers the best of both worlds in that it is a business that needs to ensure it is efficient and provides what service users want, that reinvests profits back into the organization and that engages staff by allowing them to be a shareholder within that organization. The 'John Lewis effect' suggests that engaged staff leads to better organizational perform-ance (Ellins and Ham, 2009). However, given that social enterprises may take so many different forms, some have questioned whether the government's interest in these forms is really an attempt to privatize health and social care by the backdoor.

Social enterprise is important in terms of inter-agency working as these types of organizations may span health and social care and can play an important part in providing holistic care to service users. Because social enterprise organizations sit outside of the public sector, they are not necessarily delineated by organizational and professional boundaries and therefore are not required to be described as health *or* social care agencies. However, health and social care commissioners may not always understand social enter-prises (or third sector organizations more widely) and this can lead to challenges in being chosen to deliver services. Commissioners, therefore, need to better understand social enterprises and the added value they can bring. There has also been a tendency within the NHS in particular to transfer whole services, staff groups, management teams and services out of the NHS into social enterprise – and it may be that it takes more than a change in legal status to get some of the potential benefits of this particular organizational form.

Recommendations for policy and practice

- Social enterprise is a well-established concept that is broadly concerned with adding social value through businesses. However, precise definitions vary, so it is important to be clear about what you mean when you refer to this concept.
- Social enterprise can be a way of more fully engaging staff and service users in the design and delivery of health and social care services.
- Social enterprises may offer potential for the delivery of integrated health and social care services, but it is important that commissioners understand this model and offer appropriate support to these kinds of organizations.
- Many potential benefits are claimed for social enterprise – but delivering these in practice can be difficult if we simply transfer whole services out of the public sector en masse and merely change their legal status.
- More important may be creating time and space to engage with staff and service users in order to more fully reconsider the *value* base and ethos of what is provided. By definition this may need to happen bottom-up rather than top-down and is unlikely to happen quickly.

KEY TEXTS

- Ellins, J. and Ham, C. (2009) *NHS Mutual: Engaging Staff and Aligning Incentives to Achieve Higher Levels of Performance* (London: Nuffield Trust)

  This book considers the role of mutuals in engaging NHS staff in the delivery of health and social care and the impacts this has in terms of organizational performance.

- Hunter, P. (2009) *Social Enterprise for Public Service: How Does the Third Sector Deliver?* (London: The Smith Institute)

  This monograph contains a number of chapters pertaining to different areas of public services and themes about the nature of social enterprise.

- Marks, L. and Hunter, D. (2007) *Social Enterprises and the NHS: Changing Patterns of Ownership and Accountability* (London: UNISON)

  This research report provides an account of the emergence of social enterprise in health care and the implications of these changes.

social model

SEE ALSO **long-term conditions; physical disability; values**

Historically, services for people with a *physical disability* have tended to be strongly influenced by a medical model (which sees disability as an individual, biological issue). Over time, however, this view has been increasingly challenged by groups of disabled campaigners (often described as part of an 'independent living movement') who have rejected this definition and developed a social model of disability. In this view of the world, someone may have an 'impairment' (an individual, biological condition) – but the *disability* that can result is a consequence of the discrimination that people with impairments face in this society. As an example, someone able to stand freely (who might be seen as 'able-bodied' in our current society) would actually be 'disabled' in a built environment designed for people in wheelchairs – they would have a bad back and would constantly hit their heads on low doorways. Equally, someone trying to help a person in a wheelchair who cannot reach a light switch could invest large sums of money in research to find ways of 'curing' the person – or they could simply move the light switch. Social rather than the medical, the latter intervention is much cheaper and easier – and indeed would work for everyone in a wheelchair rather than just a single individual.

Thus, disability is not a biological category but a social one (similar to the way in which the women's movement has distinguished between biological sex and socially constructed gender). As a result, the emphasis has not been on changing the individual (i.e. intervening medically to cure the individual), but on intervening to change the built environment and the way that society works. This was captured brilliantly on the front cover of a classic book by disabled academic and campaigner Mike Oliver (1990) on *The Politics of Disability*, where a person in a wheelchair is unable to reach a polling station to vote because there is a flight of steps in the way.

Two key definitions are produced by organizations of disabled people, including the following:

- *The Disabled People's International (DPI) (1982):* Impairment is the functional limitation within the individual caused by physical, mental or sensory impairment. Disability is the loss or limitation of opportunities to take part in the normal life of the community on an equal level with others due to physical and social barriers.
- *The Union of the Physically Impaired Against Segregation (UPIAS) (1976):* Impairment is lacking all or part of a limb, or having a defective limb, organ or mechanism of the body. Disability is the disadvantage or restriction of activity caused by a contemporary social organization that takes little or no account of people who have physical impairments and thus excludes them from participation in the mainstream of social activities.

Recommendations for policy and practice

- Rather than focusing on individual impairments, a social model calls for radical changes to the current political, social and economic order in order to tackle socially constructed disability.
- Like other civil rights groups, this is a campaign for equal rights and for full citizenship (rather than simply a health and social care issue).
- Such concepts have been developed by disabled people themselves, turning traditional understandings on their head and redefining the nature of the 'problem' to be solved and the potential solutions.
- A key choice for health and social care practitioners is whether they adopt the medical model that underpins many traditional services, or embrace a more radical social model.
- Although a social model is most associated with groups of people with physical impairments, it has implications for *older people*, people with *mental health* problems and people with *learning difficulties* too (see, for example, Beresford, 2000).

KEY TEXTS
- Beresford, P. (2000) 'What Have Madness and Psychiatric System Survivors Got to Do with Disability and Disability Studies?' *Disability and Society*, 15 (1): pp. 167–172

Important discussion of the implications of a social model of disability for people with mental health problems.

- French, S. and Swain, J. (2011) *Working with Disabled People in Policy and Practice: A Social Model* (Basingstoke: Palgrave Macmillan)

  Focusing specifically on health and social care, this textbook adopts a social model to develop more integrated approaches.
- For further discussion of medical and social models, key contributions are by disabled academics and campaigners such as Michael Oliver (1990, 2009; Oliver and Barnes, 1998; Oliver and Sapey, 2006). A series of early writings and material by leading disabled activists is also available free online via the Disability Archive hosted at the University of Leeds (www.leeds.ac.uk/disability-studies).

strategic collaboration

SEE partnership working

structural reform

SEE mergers and acquisitions

Sure Start

SEE area-based initiatives

synergy

SEE theory

t

teamwork

SEE ALSO co-location; culture; partnership working

Contemporary health and social care communities are confronted by complex, cross-cutting issues, but are still constrained by the structural, procedural and *cultural* barriers that are associated with a welfare system largely designed along functional lines. Against this background, effective teamwork has often been seen as one of the potential ways that we might overcome some of these challenges and provide more seamless services. Just like *leadership* and *partnership*, teamwork has also become somewhat of a buzzword in recent years and has been critiqued as being something of a management fad. Yet, when people do not work together effectively as a team, then very real and detrimental outcomes can occur. Although the term might be overused, it is so widely applied precisely because it refers to something significant. However, it does mean that we need to make an important distinction: just because we call something a team does not mean that it necessarily is – teams need investment.

So what is a team? The definitions are somewhat contested and there is debate over the size of teams, with Mueller *et al.* (2000) suggesting that a team is composed of between 3 and 15 members, although Belbin (2000) argues that the maximum size for a team is no more than 6–8 members. Given the debate over the precise size of teams, we might think about what features a group needs to be a team. Within the wider literature, the general distinction made between a team and a group is the level of inter-dependence on one another. While a group is a general collective of individuals, there needs to be more interaction and reliance between individuals for it to be a team. West and colleagues (1998) boil down the definition of a team to three criteria: the group needs to have a defined organizational function and identity; the group must possess shared objectives or goals; and team members must have inter-dependent roles.

In inter-agency settings, there are many different types of teams and the terminology can prove confusing. Therefore, we set out some of the main types of inter-agency teams and their definitions here (see also the entry on *partnership working*):

- **Multiprofessional** – practitioners who share the same professional background who practice within two or more different specialities or branches working side by side.
- **Multidisciplinary** – practitioners from two or more different disciplines working side by side.
- **Multiagency** – practitioners from two or more different agencies working side by side. The 'multi'-prefix implies that members of that group are not necessarily collaborating and might simply be working side by side, in parallel or sequentially towards a common problem. However, when the term 'team' is used as a suffix, it should imply that members are collaborating and working towards shared objectives.
- **Inter-professional** – practitioners who share the same professional background and practice within two or more different specialities or branches working together.
- **Inter-disciplinary** – practitioners from two or more different disciplines working together.
- **Inter-agency** – practitioners from two or more different agencies working together. The 'inter'-prefix denotes that there are definite interactions between the members and that there is active joint collaboration towards solving a problem – although members may not be approaching it from the same conceptual frameworks. The inter-prefix further tends to denote a greater propensity for team members to be willing to work across boundaries, which multiprofessional teams may be less willing to do. Again, whether the suffix 'team' or 'working' is used should indicate whether this collaboration is towards a specific end the members are jointly accountable for achieving.
- **Transdisciplinary teams** – members transcend their separate, conceptual and methodological orientations to overcome the disciplinary bounds that are present in multidisciplinary and

inter-disciplinary teams. Some commentators suggest that this is the only way to produce a truly integrated response to issues, although others have highlighted the dangers that might result from working in this way as this might lead to a loss of synergy.

In an inter-agency setting it is starting to be recognized that *structural reform* is not always the answer. Teamworking offers organizations a way of working flexibly and in a more agile manner. In a health and social care context, there is also some evidence that teams who work together produce better outcomes for service users, staff members and the organization (e.g. Borrill *et al.*, 2001). Working in teams can not only be beneficial in terms of service user outcomes, but can also create more satisfied team members who are more productive and more likely to enhance organizational performance. Effective teams can also create a virtuous chain of events and enhance individual and organizational performance. However, ineffective teams or those who have been insufficiently developed might turn 'toxic' and lead to negative behaviours, poor team morale and reduced effectiveness. Ultimately this means that teams need developing, supporting and investing in if they are to be effective.

In a practical sense then it is important that people understand when they are part of a team and who else is in that team. It is also important that the team has a clear task to work on, that it is meaningful for the entire team and that individuals understand the role that they play in the team. Teams need to think carefully about their knowledge, skills and abilities, and make sure that they are appropriate to the task at hand. In addition to thinking specifically about the team and its composition, the team and its composition, organizational contexts need to recognize and support team-based working if it is to be successful.

Recommendations for policy and practice
- When referring to teams, be clear what you mean by this. Just because we call something a team does not necessarily mean that it will be successful.
- There are many different types of teams that exist in inter-agency settings. Each of these have particular functions and characteristics and we would expect to achieve different types of aims and require different types of support mechanisms.

- Effective teamwork can have a positive impact on staff satisfaction, organizational outcomes and patient outcomes. However, dysfunctional teams might produce 'toxic' environments, which can be detrimental for both staff and services users.
- Teams need investment and development in order to be successful.

KEY TEXTS

- Jelphs, K. and Dickinson, H. (2008) *Working in Teams* (Bristol: The Policy Press)

  Offers a summary of the literature relating to teamworking in an inter-agency context.

- West, M. (2012) *Effective Teamwork: Practical Lessons from Organisational Research.* 3rd edn (Oxford: Blackwell Publishing)

  A helpful practical insight into teamwork based on high-quality research from a health context.

- West, M. and Markiewicz, L. (2004) *Building Team-based Working: A Practical Guide to Organizational Transformation* (Oxford: British Psychological Society/Blackwell Publishing)

  A helpful guide for those who are thinking of building effective teams.

theory

SEE ALSO evaluation; partnership working

Dickinson (2008) argues that the field of inter-agency working is under-theorized and relies mainly on descriptive accounts of what individuals and groups have done and how they have worked together in practice. Theories are essentially short-hands for understanding and explaining particular situations and making predictions about what might happen and why. They are analytical tools that abstract to a macro-level to help people understand contexts and predict their actions. Yet, despite accounts of inter-agency working often being under-theorized, this does not mean that there is not a wealth of different theoretical models that might be drawn upon.

Sullivan and Skelcher (2002) explore the range of different theoretical models that there are to explain why it is that partners might seek to work together and what this should produce. These authors have produced a framework to organize these various theoretical perspectives of joint working according to whether they represent 'optimistic', 'pessimistic' or 'realistic' perspectives of collaboration (this is listed in Table 2).

Optimist perspectives of collaboration tend to be characterized as those which presuppose consensus and shared vision between partners. Optimistic perspectives suggest that partners collaborate to produce positive results for the entire system and predominantly for altruistic purposes. One example ascribed to this perspective is 'Exchange Theory' (Levine and White, 1962). This suggests that by working together organizations may achieve more than they may do separately – that is 'collaborative advantage' or 'synergy' (see below for further discussion of this concept). Organizations collaborate as they are dependent on each other for resources and in order to achieve their overall goals or objectives.

	Optimist	Pessimist	Realist
Why collabora-tion happens	Achieving shared vision: *Collaborative empowerment theory, Regime theory* Resource maximization: *Exchange theory*	Maintaining/ enhancing position: *Resource dependency theory*	Responding to new environments: *Evolutionary theory*
What form of collaboration is developed and why	Multiple relationships: *Collaborative empow-erment theory*	Inter-organizational network: *Resource dependency theory*	Formalized networks: *Evolutionary theory* Policy networks as governance instruments: *Policy networks theories*

TABLE 2   *Optimist, pessimist and realist theories of collaboration*
Source: Adapted from Sullivan and Skelcher (2002, p. 36).

Pessimistic perspectives of collaboration predict that organizations or agencies will only enter into such arrangements if they will enhance their own gain or power above anything else. In other words, the process of collaboration will only occur if it is in the mutual interest of each party to try control or influence the other's activities. One example of this pessimistic approach is 'Resource-dependency Theory', which proposes that actors lacking in essential resources will seek to establish relationships with (i.e. be dependent upon) others in order to obtain needed resources (Emerson, 1962). Organizations might also try to change their dependence relationships by reducing how dependent they are on other organizations or how many others are dependent on them.

Realist perspectives are a more nuanced view of the reasons why collaboration might exist than the two outlined above, suggesting that in response to the wider environment, both altruism and individual gain may coexist. What is important in this perspective is how organizations change in response to the wider environment and how they might achieve gains through collaboration. An example of this comes in the form of 'New Institutional Treaty', and Dickinson and Glasby (2010) employ this framework in explaining the appeal of partnership working in health and social care. DiMaggio and Powell (1991) suggest that the emergent belief system about organizations supersedes any possible beliefs about the most effective of ways of arranging particular organizational aspects. In so doing they refer to the phenomenon of 'institutional morphism', which suggests that particular initiatives or characteristics are taken on by organizations due to the value ascribed to them within their normative environments. In other words, organizations take on particular characteristics or initiatives, not because they have necessarily demonstrated that they are the most effective, but because the institutional environment values these behaviours. This is of particular interest in relation to collaboration, given that partnerships are internationally being recognized as answers to the problem of service improvement in a number of areas – despite lacking a clear empirical underpinning.

As we indicated above, inter-agency collaboration is often predicated on the basis that it should produce something that is 'greater than the sum of its parts'. Mackintosh (1992) provides a helpful distinction between three different types of *outcome* that a partnership may be trying to achieve:

- **Synergy** (bringing together partners with different assets and powers to create something where the whole is greater than the sum of its parts).
- **Transformation** (bringing partners together to change the objectives and *culture* of one or both of the organizations, with the direction of change depending on the *power* of each individual partner).
- **Budget enlargement** (coming together to try to obtain a financial contribution from a third party).

These concepts were further developed by Hastings (1996), who suggests that synergy is either produced by

- The extra power that is attained by bringing together resources (e.g. economies of scale/bargaining power).
- More innovation and creativity through bringing together different perspectives.

Putting these concepts together we find that 'resource synergy' occurs where there is co-operation and co-ordination over the spending of resources and this should lead to added value from the resources spent, for example, increased effectiveness or efficiency. 'Policy synergy' occurs where joint approaches are developed through combining the different perspectives of each partner, which should lead to the creation of new perspectives and innovative solutions (Hastings, 1996). Using these categories, perhaps one of the reasons why collaborations sometimes seem to fail to deliver ambitious aspirations is that service users are seeking the benefits of 'policy synergy', while managers are seeking 'resource synergy'.

Recommendations for policy and practice
- There are a range of different theories that suggest different rationales, drivers and expected results for inter-agency working.
- Yet, theories are not very widely used in the field of health and social care inter-agency working. More explicitly drawing on

these models might help individuals and groups to be more clear about why they think collaborative working is important.

- Groups might engage in collaborative arrangements for the good of others, due to self-interest or due to a dynamic interaction of different factors.
- There are a range of potential outcomes or aims of joint working according to different schools of thought, and it is important to be clear what outcomes joint working might be expected to achieve.

KEY TEXTS

- Dickinson, H. (2008) *Evaluating Outcomes in Health and Social Care* (Bristol: The Policy Press)

  This text applies various theories of collaboration to a health and social care context.

- Hastings, A. (1996) 'Unravelling the Process of "Partnership" in Urban Regeneration Policy', *Urban Studies*, 33: pp. 253–268

  This paper includes a helpful analysis of the models of synergy.

- Sullivan, H. and Skelcher, C. (2002) *Working across Boundaries: Collaboration in Public Services* (Basingstoke: Palgrave Macmillan)

  This book provides a comprehensive and accessible introduction to the range of theories that underpin collaboration.

theory-led approaches

SEE **evaluation**

third sector

SEE **mixed economy of care**

transdisciplinary working

SEE **partnership working**

trust

SEE ALSO **co-location; communication; culture; inter-professional education; leadership; values**

As we have argued throughout other entries in this book, much of the literature on health and social care partnerships has a tendency to be quite descriptive in nature, recording how different individuals and organizations interact with one another. In these descriptive accounts of inter-agency working one of the factors that is often identified as being important is that of trust. As an example of this Cameron and Lart (2003, p. 13) state that 'key ingredients to successful joint working are trust and respect. To be successful, organizations and the personnel working within them must trust and respect the work of partner agencies and/or partner professionals.' The old saying that 'trust is hard to build but easy to destroy' rings out as a warning message in many of these accounts.

The theme of trust – and its obverse distrust – appear consistently through accounts of inter-agency working and there are similarities with the notion of *partnership working* itself: both are words that appear frequently; both seem to be treated unquestioningly as a 'good thing' and neither tend to be defined in a systematic way when they are used. To some extent, this is perhaps unsurprising in the sense that we all have a general understanding of what trust is and probably often use this term in our everyday lives. Yet, trust is a tricky term conceptually and there is vast amount of scholarly material that seeks to explain it, making it all the more challenging to be definitive about what it means in the context of inter-agency working. In the next section, we provide a brief overview of some of the 'confusing potpourri of definitions' (Shapiro, 1987, p. 624) that have been applied to the concept of trust and then go on to illustrate some of the ways that trust might be important in terms of an inter-agency context.

One way of thinking about different definitions of trust is to group them via disciplinary perspectives. Lewicki and Bunker (1995) group these into personality theorists' view of trust as individual difference; sociologists and economists' sense of trust as an institutional entity; and social psychologists' notion of trust as an expectation of another party in a transaction. As we will see below, each of these different disciplinary notions of trust is present in the inter-agency literature. Sitkin and Roth (1993) define trust not by a disciplinary perspective but in the categories of trust as an individual attribute; trust as behaviour; trust as a situational feature; and trust as an institutional arrangement. What these attempts to make sense of this concept suggest is that trust is multifaceted and there are many different types of trust. Indeed, rather than asking 'what is trust', Bigley and Pearce (1998) suggest a better question is 'which trust and when' (p. 406).

On one level, trust essentially involves knowing that your partner (either at an institutional or individual level) will essentially fulfil their part of the bargain and any efforts expended by one party on behalf of another will ultimately be reciprocated in some way. Trust also involves knowing that your partner will not do anything untoward, which might be damaging to you, again as either an individual or an institution. As suggested above, this notion of trust may take a number of different forms depending on the particular context. At an institutional level the different modes of *governance* (i.e. *hierarchy*, *market* or *network*) each have different expectations in terms of trust, whether this is trust in the system of *power*, trust in contracts or trust in relationships.

One of the sources of distrust often cited in inter-agency settings is that of misunderstanding. Where individuals and organizations do not fully understand either the roles or *values* of particular partner agencies and/or partner professionals, this can lead to problems of trust (Cameron and Lart, 2003). Where this level of understanding is absent, there may be suspicions over the motives or the approaches of partners. An example of this might be the different approaches to notions of care that health and social care partners might hold (Wistow and Waddington, 2006), different professional working practices (Ross and Tissier, 1997) or different levels of professional autonomy (Cameron and Lart, 2003). Where individuals work in inter-agency settings away from their traditional organizational or professional base, they may feel isolated, misunderstood or as though their loyalties are divided.

There are other more structural or systematic sources of trust and distrust, which might also impact on inter-agency working. One that is prominent in health and social care is that of frequent reorganization. Where one partner organization has been subject to frequent changes, it may lead to other partners not being as willing to enter into collaborative endeavours for fear that these may be broken down by possible future changes. Similarly, if one partner is under financial or budgetary pressures, another may be wary of entering into joint working arrangements for fear of being left having to pick up the costs.

Recommendations for policy and practice

- Trust is a complex and multifaceted factor that may be gained and lost through a variety of different mechanisms.
- Trust is thought to be a helpful factor in promoting inter-agency working and partners may look to improve levels of trust to improve their collaborative endeavours.
- Trust is a concept that may mean a multitude of different things, so when we use this term, it is helpful if we can be clear about what we mean by it at that time and in that particular place.
- Misunderstanding or a lack of understanding can be a key source of distrust in partner agencies and/or professionals.
- Constant structural change and financial problems can be two common sources of mistrust between partner agencies.

KEY TEXTS

- Cameron, A. and Lart, R. (2003) 'Factors Promoting and Obstacles Hindering Joint Working: A Systematic Review of the Research Evidence', *Journal of Integrated Care*, 11: pp. 9–17

  This article provides an overview of the many ways in which trust and distrust may be manifest in inter-agency settings. The original study has since been updated by Cameron *et al.* (2012), with a specific focus on older people and mental health.

- Kramer, R.M. and Tyler, T.R. (1995) *Trust in Organizations: Frontiers of Theory and Research* (Thousand Oaks: Sage)

  This text provides an overview of many of the different approaches to understanding trust in the context of organizational research.

values

SEE ALSO culture; trust

Pendleton and King (2002, p. 1325) define values as 'deeply held views that act as guiding principles for individuals and organisations.' Values are often hidden, or rather invisible, but they can be crucial in either facilitating close inter-agency working or else prove to be a barrier in attempts at joint working. Waine *et al.* (2005, p. 11) describe values as 'taken-for-granted meanings'. Where individuals and agencies have worked together for a significant length of time, these will be understood and partners will be able to predict and *trust* the actions of their collaborators. Where the values of partners are not understood, this can lead to distrust and uncertainty. Much of the discussion that is presented here links to the concept of *culture*, which is, in part at least, informed by values (and readers who are interested in the concept of values may wish to also read the *culture* entry to gain a more rounded view).

Individuals and organizations are not always very explicit about their values and to some extent we might think it a bit odd if, on a first meeting with someone, they started to tell us about their value base. However, values are important in guiding our actions and we are more likely to trust someone else who shares our values. Many commercial sector organizations nowadays go out of their way to tell us what their values are. Research evidence suggests that where organizations are explicit about values and use these in a very real way to underpin and guide their actions, these organizations tend to outperform others significantly (Collins and Porras, 1994).

Traditionally, health and social care have had different values – and this can make joint working challenging. While health is individually focused with the professional as expert and might be generally described as paternalistic, social care in more group-focused, with the professional as facilitator and social care is more often described as empowering. Where the values of partners come into conflict, this can lead to difficulties in attempts to work jointly as partners may not understand why their colleagues act in particular ways. We can see this in a variety of different areas, but we will focus on two here: one from adult care and another from children's services.

The first example is of criminal justice agencies working jointly with mental health staff. In this case study, the values of the criminal justice agency primarily related to protecting the general population from potentially dangerous individuals, while mental health staff were much more used to the protection of vulnerable individuals. At the heart of the problem was the degree to which the partners took responsibility for the problems and solutions associated with offenders with mental health problems – with neither partner consistently taking responsibility for either at the start of the process. As Cruser and Diamond (1996) report, differing value bases caused difficulties in the abilities of partners to interact with each other in being able to understand one another or deal with each other's different aims and approaches. However, this was able to be overcome through organizational development interventions.

The next example of a clash of values is taken from a children's service setting and involves social work and education partners. Where a child is taken into care, they may have associated behavioural issues that are manifest in educational settings. These may prove to be disruptive to other students and teachers may be keen to exclude individuals from classrooms for the good of other pupils. Despite acknowledging the importance of educational attainment, social workers might oppose this and be keen to keep disruptive individuals in a school environment as the social elements of this can be helpful in supporting children through difficult times. Here the clash of values between educational attainment and care for an individual child can pose difficulties for professionals trying to work together to best support this child (Beckett and Maynard, 2005).

Recommendations for policy and practice
- Values can play an important part in the success of inter-agency collaboration and not paying attention to values can lead to difficulties in joint working practices.
- Where values are declared and followed in practice, they can produce trust between individuals and organizations.

- Where values are declared but not followed, then this can cause distrust between partners.
- Where values are not stated, this can lead to members of organizations or potential partner organizations being unclear about what an entity stands for.
- Organizational development interventions can be employed to help partners retain their value bases but work together more effectively.

KEY TEXTS

- Beckett, C. and Maynard, A. (2005) *Values and Ethics in Social Work: An Introduction* (London: Sage)

  This text provides an introduction to values in the context of social work practice.

- Cruser, D.A. and Diamond, P.M. (1996) 'An Exploration of Social Policy and Organizational Culture in Jail-based Mental Health Services', *Administration and Policy in Mental Health*, 24: pp. 129–148

  This paper explores the conflicts between criminal justice and mental health partners in practice.

- Waine, B. *et al.* (2005) *Developing Social Care: Values and Principles* (London: Social Care Institute for Excellence)

  This report summarizes evidence about the kinds of principles and values that underpin social care in a British context.

voluntary sector

SEE **mixed economy of care**

whole systems working

SEE partnership working

references

Alakeson, V. (2007) *The Case for Extending Self-Direction in the NHS* (London, Social Market Foundation)

Alakeson, V. (2011) *The Active Patient* (Birmingham, Health Services Management Centre/Centre for Welfare Reform)

Allen, K. and Glasby, J. (2010) '"The Billion Dollar Question": Embedding Prevention in Older People's Services – 10 High Impact Changes', Policy Paper 8 (Birmingham, HSMC)

Allen, R., Gilbert, P. and Onyett, S. (2009) *Leadership for Personalisation and Social Inclusion in Mental Health* (London, Social Care Institute for Excellence)

Allen, P. *et al.* (2011) *Investigating the Governance of NHS Foundation Trusts* (NIHR: SDO programme) (project 08/1618/157)

Arnstein, S. (1969) 'A Ladder of Citizen Participation', *Journal of the American Institute of Planners*, 35 (4): pp. 216–224

Arrow, K.J. (1974) *The Limits of Organization* (New York: Norton)

Association of Directors of Adult Social Services (ADASS) (2008) '*Mental Health into the Mainstream*', www.adass.org.uk [accessed 29/08/2008)]

Association of Directors of Social Services (2005) *Safeguarding Adults: A National Framework of Standards for Good Practice and Outcomes* (London: ADSS)

Atwal, A. and Caldwell, K. (2002) 'Do Multidisciplinary Integrated Care Pathways Improve Interprofessional Collaboration?' *Scandinavian Journal Caring Sciences*, 16: pp. 360–367

Audit Commission (2009) *Means to an End: Joint Financing across Health and Social Care* (London: Audit Commission)

Audit Commission (2011) *Joining up Health and Social Care: Improving Value for Money across the Interface* (London: Audit Commission)

Axford, N. and Berry, V. (2005) 'Measuring Outcomes in the "New" Children's Services', *Journal of Integrated Care*, 13: pp. 12–23.

Bachman, M. *et al.* (2009) 'Integrating Children's Services in England: National Evaluation of Children's Trusts', *Child: Care, Health and Development*, 35 (2): pp. 257–265

Baggott, R. (2010) *Public Health: Policy and Politics.* 2nd edn (Basingstoke: Palgrave Macmillan)

Barnes, M. *et al.* (2005) *Health Action Zones: Partnerships for Health Equity* (London: Routledge)

Barr, H. (2002) *Interprofessional Education Today, Yesterday and Tomorrow: A Review* (London: Centre for the Advancement of Inter professional Education/Learning and Teaching Support Network for Health Sciences and Practice)

Barr, H. *et al.* (2005) *Effective Interprofessional Education: Argument, Assumption and Evidence* (Oxford: Blackwell Publishing)

Barton, P. *et al.* (2005) *A National Evaluation of the Costs and Outcomes of Intermediate Care for Older People* (Birmingham/Leicester: Health Services Management Centre/Nuffield Community Care Studies Unit)

Baskin, K., Goldstein, J. and Lindberg, C. (2000) 'Merging, De-merging, and Emerging at Deaconess Billings Clinic', *Physician Executive*, 26: pp. 20–26

Bate, P. (1995) *Strategies for Cultural Change* (Oxford: Butterworth-Heinemann)

Beckett, C. and Maynard, A. (2005) *Values and Ethics in Social Work: An Introduction* (London: Sage)

Belbin, M. (2000) *Beyond the Team* (Oxford, Butterworth-Heinemann)

Bell, D. and Bowes, A. (2006) *Financial Care Models in Scotland and the UK: A Review of the Introduction of Free Personal Care for Older People in Scotland* (York: Joseph Rowntree Foundation)

Belsky, J., Barnes, J. and Melhuish, E.C. (eds) (2007) *The National Evaluation of Sure Start: Does Area-Based Early Intervention Work?* (Bristol: The Policy Press)

Bennis, W.G. (1994) *On Becoming a Leader* (New York: Perseus Press)

Beresford, P. (2000) 'What Have Madness and Psychiatric System Survivors Got to Do with Disability and Disability Studies?' *Disability and Society*, 15 (1): pp. 167–172

Berridge, V. (1999) *Health and Society in Britain Since 1939* (Cambridge: Cambridge University Press)

Bevan, G. and Hood, C. (2006) 'What's Measured Is What Matters: Targets and Gaming in the English Health Care System', *Public Administration*, 84: pp. 517–538

Bigley, G.A. and Pearce, J.L. (1998) 'Straining for Shared Meaning in Organization Science: Problems of Trust and Distrust', *Academy of Management Review*, 23 (3): pp. 405–421

Blinkhorn, M. (2004) *Social Worker: Leading Roles in Mental Health – Adjustment to Change, New Ways of Working and Other Potential Solutions* (Durham: Northern Centre for Mental Health)

Bolden, R. and Gosling, J. (2006) 'Is the NHS Leadership Qualities Framework Missing the Wood for the Trees?' in A. Casbeer, A. Harrison and A. Mark (eds), *Innovations in Health Care: A Reality Check* (Basingstoke: Palgrave Macmillan)

Borrill, C. *et al.* (2001) *The Effectiveness of Health Care Teams in the National Health Service* (Birmingham: Aston Centre for Health Service Organization Research)

Boyle, D. (2004) 'Is This How to End Public Service Failure?' *New Statesman*, 133: pp. 2–21

Boyle, D. *et al.* (2010) *Right Here, Right Now: Taking Co-Production into the Mainstream* (London: NESTA)

Bragato, L. and Jacobs, K. (2003) 'Care Pathways: The Road to Better Health Services?' *Journal of Health Organization and Management*, 17 (3): pp. 164–180

Braithwaite, J., Runciman, W.B. and Merry, A.F. (2009) 'Towards Safer, Better Healthcare: Harnessing the Natural Properties of Complex Sociotechnical Systems', *Quality and Safety in Health Care*, 18 (1): pp. 37–41.

Broadhurst, K., Grover, C. and Jamieson, J. (2009) *Critical Perspectives on Safeguarding Children* (Oxford: Wiley)

Brodie, D. (2004) 'Partnership Working: A Service User Perspective', in J. Glasby and E. Peck (eds), *Care Trusts: Partnership Working in Action* (Abingdon: Radcliffe Medical Press)

Brown, L., Tucker, C. and Domokos, T. (2003) 'Evaluating the Impact of Integrated Health and Social Care Teams on Older People Living in the Community', *Health and Social Care in the Community*, 11: pp. 85–94

Bryan, S. *et al.* (2002) 'The Role of Integrated Care Pathways in Improving the Client Experience', *Professional Nurse*, 18 (2): pp. 77–79

Buckner, L. and Yeandle, S. (2011) *Valuing Carers 2011: Calculating the Value of Carers' Support* (London: Carers UK)

Calman-Hine Report (1995) *A Policy Framework for Commissioning Cancer Services* (London: Department of Health)

Cambridge, P. and Carnaby, S. (eds) (2005) *Person-Centred Planning and Care Management with People with Learning Disabilities* (London: Jessica Kingsley)

Cameron, A. and Lart, R. (2003) 'Factors Promoting and Obstacles Hindering Joint Working: A Systematic Review of the Research Evidence', *Journal of Integrated Care*, 11: pp. 9–17

Cameron, A. *et al.* (2012) *Factors That Promote and Hinder Joint and Integrated Working between Health and Social Care Services* (London: SCIE)

Carers UK (2004) *In Poor Health: The Impact of Caring on Health* (London: Carers UK)

Carers UK (2005) *Facts about Carers* (London: Carers UK)

Carers UK (2010) *Looking after Someone: A Guide to Carers' Rights and Benefits 2010/11* (London: Carers UK)

Carleton, R.J. (1997) 'Cultural Due Diligence', *Training*, 34: pp. 67–80.

Carpenter, J. and Dickinson, H. (2008) *Interprofessional Education and Training* (Bristol: The Policy Press)

Clegg, S. (1989) *Frameworks of Power* (London: Sage)

Clegg, S., Kornberger, M. and Pitsis, T. (2005) *Managing and Organizations: An Introduction to Theory and Practice* (London: Sage)

Clements, L. (2011) *Carers and Their Rights – The Law Relating to Carers*. 4th edn (London: Carers UK)

Collins, J. and Porras, J. (1994) *Built to Last: Successful Habits of Visionary Companies* (New York: Harper Business)

Connell, J.P. *et al.* (eds) (1995) *New Approaches to Evaluating Community Initiatives: Concepts, Methods, and Contexts* (New York: The Aspen Institute)

Connolly, S., Bevan, G. and Mays, N. (2010) *Funding and Performance of Healthcare Systems in the Four Countries of the UK before and after Devolution* (London: The Nuffield Trust)

Contandripoulos, D. *et al.* (2004) 'Governance Structures and Political Processes in a Public System: Lessons from Quebec', *Public Administration*, 82: pp. 627–655

Corrigan, P. and Mitchell, C. (2011) *The Hospital Is Dead, Long Live the Hospital* (London: Reform)

Coulter, A. and Ellins, J. (2006) *Patient-Focused Interventions: A Review of Evidence* (London: The Health Foundation)

Crisp, N. (2011) *24 Hours to Save the NHS* (Oxford: Oxford University Press)

Cruser, D.A. and Diamond, P.M. (1996) 'An Exploration of Social Policy and Organizational Culture in Jail-based Mental Health Services', *Administration and Policy in Mental Health*, 24: pp. 129–148

Cummins, J. and Miller, C. (2007) *Co-production and Social Capital* (London: OPM)

Curry, N. and Ham, C. (2010) *Clinical and Service Integration: The Route to Improved Outcomes* (London: King's Fund)

Davey, B. *et al.* (2005) 'Integrating Health and Social Care: Implications for Joint Working and Community Care Outcomes for Older People', *Journal of Interprofessional Care*, 19: pp. 22–34

Davies, J.S. (2011) *Challenging Governance Theory: From Networks to Hegemony* (Bristol: The Policy Press)

Deakin, N. (2001) *In Search of Civil Society* (Basingstoke: Palgrave Macmillan)

Department for Communities and Local Government (2010) *The New Deal for Communities Programme: Achieving a Neighbourhood Focus for Regeneration* (London, DCLG)

Department for Communities and Local Government (2011) *Long Term Evaluation of Local Area Agreements and Local Strategic Partnerships 2007–2010: Final Report* (London: DCLG)

Department for Education and Skills (2003) *Every Child Matters: Change for Children* (London: HMSO)

Department of Health (1998) *Partnership in Action: New Opportunities for Joint Working between Health and Social Services – a Discussion Document* (London: Department of Health)

Department of Health (2000) *The NHS Plan: A Plan for Investment, a Plan for Reform* (London: TSO)

Department of Health (2001a) *National Service Framework for Older People: Modern Standards and Service Models* (London: Department of Health)

Department of Health (2001b) *Intermediate Care* (HSC 2001/001, LAC (2001)1)

Department of Health (2001c) *Valuing People: A New Strategy for Learning Disability for the 21st Century* (London: TSO)

Department of Health (2003a) *Confidentiality: NHS Code of Practice* (London: Department of Health)

Department of Health (2003b) *Discharge from Hospital: Pathway, Process and Practice* (London: Department of Health) (accessible, step-by-step good practice guidance)

Department of Health (2004) *Chronic Disease Management: A Compendium of Information* (London: Department of Health)

Department of Health (2005) *National Service Framework for Long-term Conditions* (London: Department of Health)

Department of Health (2006a) *Our Health, Our Care, Our Say: A New Direction for Community Services* (London: TSO)

Department of Health (2006b) *Supporting People with Long Term Conditions to ... Self-care: A Guide to Developing Local Strategies and Good Practice* (London: Department of Health)

Department of Health (2007a) *World Class Commissioning: Vision* (London: Department of Health)

Department of Health (2007b) *Guidance on Joint Strategic Needs Assessment* (London: Department of Health)

Department of Health (2008) *Real Involvement: Working with People to Improve Health Services* (London: Department of Health)

Department of Health (2009) *The National Framework for NHS Continuing Healthcare and NHS-funded Nursing Care, July 2009. Revised* (London: Department of Health)

Department of Health (2010a) *Equity and Excellence: Liberating the NHS* (London: TSO)

Department of Health (2010b) *Transforming Community Services: An Intro-duction to the Programme*, Government slides available online via: www. dh.gov.uk/en/Healthcare/TCS/index.htm.

Department of Health (2011a) *Transforming Community Services Transfor-mational Guides*, series of guides to transforming various community services available online via http://www.dh.gov.uk/en/Publicati onsand-statistics/Publications/PublicationsPolicyAndGuidance /DH_124178)

Department of Health (2011b) *The New Public Health System: Summary* (London: Department of Health)

Department of Health (2012) *Performance and Capability Review: Care Quality Commission* (London: Department of Health)

Department of Trade and Industry (2002) *Social Enterprise: A Strategy for Success* (London: DTI)

Dewar, S. (2003) *Government and the NHS – Time for a New Relationship?* (London: King's Fund)

Dickinson, H. (2008) *Evaluating Outcomes in Health and Social Care* (Bristol: The Policy Press)

Dickinson, H. and Glasby, J. (2010) 'Why Partnership Working Doesn't Work', *Public Management Review*, 12: pp. 811–828

Dickinson, H. and Nicholds, A. (2012) 'The Impact of Joint Commis-sioning' in J. Glasby (ed.), *Commissioning for Health and Well-being: An Introduction* (Bristol: The Policy Press)

Dickinson, H., Peck, E. and Smith, J. (2006) *Leadership in Organisational Transition – What Can We Learn from Research Evidence? Summary Report* (Birmingham: Health Services Management Centre)

Dickinson, H. *et al.* (2007) 'Free Personal Care in Scotland: A Narrative Review', *British Journal of Social Work*, 37: pp. 459–474

Dickinson, H. *et al.* (2013) *Joint Commissioning in Health and Social Care: An Exploration of Definitions, Processes, Services and Outcomes* (Birmingham: Health Services Management Centre) (for the NHS Health Service Research and Delivery programme)

Dilnot, A. (2011) *Fairer Care Funding: The Report of the Commission on Funding of Care and Support* (The Dilnot Review), via https: //www. wp.dh.gov.uk/carecommission/files/2011/07/Fairer-Care-Funding-Re-port.pdf [accessed 25/11/11]

DiMaggio, P.J. and Powell, W.W. (1991) *The New Institutionalism in Organi-zational Analysis* (London: University of Chicago Press)

Disabled People's International (1982) *Disabled People's International: Proceedings of the First World Congress* (Singapore: Disabled People's International)

Dore, R. (1973) *British Factory-Japanese Factory* (Berkley: University of California)

Dow, J. (2005) 'Data Sharing: An Introduction', *Journal of Integrated Care*, 13 (3), pp. 11–13

Drakeford, M. (1999) *Social Policy and Privatisation* (Harlow: Pearson)

Duffy, S. (2003) *Keys to Citizenship: A Guide to Getting Good Support for People with Learning Disabilities* (Birkenhead: Paradigm)

Durkheim, E. (1933) *The Division of Labor in Society* (New York: Free Press)

Edwards, M. and Miller, C. (2003) *Integrating Health and Social Care and Making It Work* (London: Office for Public Management)

Edwards, A. *et al.* (2006) *Working to Prevent the Social Exclusion of Young People: Final Lessons from the National Evaluation of the Children's Fund* (London: Department for Education and Skills)

Edwards, N. (2010) *The Triumph of Hope over Experience: Lessons from the History of Reorganisation* (London: NHS Confederation)

Ellins, J. (2012) 'Public and User Involvement in Commissioning' in J. Glasby (ed.), *Commissioning for Health and Well-being* (Bristol: The Policy Press)

Ellins, J. and Glasby, J. (2008) *Implementing Joint Strategic Needs Assessment: Pitfalls, Possibilities and Progress* (Leeds: Integrated Care Network/ Health Services Management Centre)

Ellins, J. and Ham, C. (2009) *NHS Mutual: Engaging Staff and Aligning Incentives to Achieve Higher Levels of Performance* (London: Nuffield Trust)

Emerson, E. *et al.* (2010) *People with Learning Disabilities in England 2010* (Lancaster: Learning Disabilities Public Health Observatory, University of Lancaster)

Emerson, R.M. (1962) 'Power Dependence Relations', *American Sociological Review*, 27: pp. 31–40

Farnsworth, A. (2012) 'Unintended Consequences? The Impact of NHS Reforms upon Torbay Care Trust', *Journal of Integrated Care*, 20 (3): pp. 146–151

Ferlie, E. *et al.* (1996) *The New Public Management in Action* (Oxford: Oxford University Press)

Ferlie, E. *et al.* (2010) *Networks in Health Care: A Comparative Study of Their Management, Impact and Performance* (Report for the National Institute for Health Research Service Delivery and Organisation Programme, SDO Project) (08/1518/102) (London: Department of Management, Kings College London)

Finch, J. (2000) 'Interprofessional Education and Teamworking: A View from Educational Providers', *British Medical Journal*, 321: pp. 1138–1140.

Foundation Trust Network (2006) *Foundation Trusts: Two Years On* (London: Foundation Trust Network)

French, S. and Swain, J. (2011) *Working with Disabled People in Policy and Practice: A Social Model* (Basingstoke: Palgrave Macmillan)

Freeth, D. *et al.* (2005) *Effective Interprofessional Education: Development, Delivery and Evaluation* (Oxford: Blackwell Publishing)

Fulop, N. *et al.* (2011) 'Implementing Changes to Hospital Services: Factors Influencing the Process and "Results" of Reconfiguration', *Health Policy*, 104 (2), pp. 128–135

Giddens, A. (1984) *The Constitution of Society* (Cambridge: Polity Press)

Glasby, J. (2003) *Hospital Discharge: Integrating Health and Social Care* (Abingdon: Radcliffe Medical Press)

Glasby, J. (2005) 'The Integration Dilemma: How Deep and How Broad to Go?' *Journal of Integrated Care*, 13 (5): pp. 27–30

Glasby, J. (ed.) (2012a) *Commissioning for Health and Well-Being: An Introduction* (Bristol: The Policy Press)

Glasby, J. (2012b) *Understanding Health and Social Care.* 2nd edn (Bristol: The Policy Press)

Glasby, J. and Dickinson, H. (2008) *Partnership Working in Health and Social Care* (Bristol: The Policy Press)

Glasby, J. and Littlechild, R. (2004) *The Health and Social Care Divide: The Experiences of Older People.* 2nd edn (Bristol: The Policy Press)

Glasby, J. and Littlechild, R. (2009) *Direct Payments and Personal Budgets: Putting Personalisation into Practice.* 2nd edn (Bristol: The Policy Press)

Glasby, J. and Peck, E. (eds) (2004) *Care Trusts: Partnership Working in Action* (Abingdon: Radcliffe Medical Press)

Glasby, J. *et al.* (2007) *'Things Can Only Get Better?' – The Argument for NHS Independence* (Birmingham: Health Services Management Centre)

Glasby, J. *et al.* (2010) *The Case for Social Care Reform – The Wider Economic and Social Benefits* (for the Department of Health/Downing Street) (Birmingham: HSMC/Institute of Applied Social Studies)

Glendinning, C., Hudson, B. and Means, R. (2005) 'Under Strain? Exploring the Troubled Relationship between Health and Social Care', *Public Money and Management*, 25: pp. 245–251

Glendinning, C., Powell, M. and Rummery, K. (eds) (2002) *Partnerships, New Labour and the Governance of Welfare* (Bristol: The Policy Press)

Glendinning, C. *et al.* (2002) *National Evaluation of Notifications for the Use of the Section 31 Partnership Flexibilities in the Health Act 1999: Final Project Report* (Leeds/Manchester: Nuffield Institute for Health / National Primary Care Research and Development Centre)

Glendinning C. *et al.* (2006) *Outcomes-Focused Services for Older People* (London: SCIE)

Glendinning, C. *et al.* (2008) *Evaluation of the Individual Budgets Pilot Programme* (York: Social Policy Research Unit)

Godfrey, M. *et al.* (2005) *An Evaluation of Intermediate Care for Older People: Final Report* (Leeds: Institute of Health Sciences and Public Health Research)

Godfrey, M. *et al.* (2008) *Reimbursement in Practice: The Last Piece of the Jigsaw? A Comparative Study of Delayed Hospital Discharge in England and Scotland* (Stirling: Leeds and London, University of Stirling, University of Leeds, King's College London)

Goodwin, N. *et al.* (2004) *Managing across Diverse Networks of Care: Lessons from Other Sectors* (London: NHS Service Delivery and Organisation R&D programme)

Gorsky, M. (2007) 'Local Leadership in Public Health: The Role of the Medical Officer of Health in Britain, 1872–1974', *Journal of Epidemiology and Community Health*, 61 (6): pp. 468–472

Greer, S.L. (2008) 'Devolution and Divergence in UK Health Policies', *British Medical Journal*, 337: p. a2616

Grint, K. (2005) *Leadership: Limits and Possibilities* (Basingstoke: Palgrave Macmillan)

Ham, C. and Hunt, P. (2008) *Membership Governance in NHS Foundation Trusts: A Review for the Department of Health* (Birmingham/London: Health Services Management Centre/Mutuo)

Ham, C. and Singh, D. (2006) *Improving Care for People with Long-term Conditions: A Review of UK and International Frameworks* (Birmingham: Health Services Management Centre)

Harris, J., Piper, S. and Morgan, H. (2003) *Experiences of Providing Care to People with Long-term Conditions: Full Report* (York: Social Policy Research Unit)

Harrison, A. *et al.* (1992) *Just Managing: Power and Culture in the NHS* (Basingstoke: Macmillan)

Hastings, A. (1996) 'Unravelling the Process of "Partnership" in Urban Regeneration Policy', *Urban Studies*, 33: pp. 253–268

Health Foundation (2011) *Helping People Help Themselves: A Review of the Evidence Considering Whether It Is Worthwhile to Support Self-Management* (London: Health Foundation)

Health Select Committee (1996) *Long-Term Care: Future Provision and Funding – Third Report, Session 1995–1996, Vol. 1* (London: HMSO)

Heath, H. and Watson, R. (eds) (2005) *Older People: Assessment for Health and Social Care* (London: Age Concern England)

Heenan, D. and Birrell, D. (2006) 'The Integration of Health and Social Care: The Lessons from Northern Ireland', *Social Policy and Administration*, 40: pp. 47–66

Heenan, D. and Birrell, D. (2009) 'Organisational Integration in Health and Social Care: Some Reflections on the Northern Ireland Experience', *Journal of Integrated Care*, 17 (5): pp. 3–12

Henwood, M. (1998) *Ignored and Invisible? Carers' Experience of the NHS* (London: Carers National Association)

Henwood, M. (2004) *Reimbursement and Delayed Discharges* (Leeds: Integrated Care Network)

Henwood, M. (2006) 'Effective Partnership Working: A Case Study of Hospital Discharge', *Health and Social Care in the Community*, 14 (5), pp. 400–7

Henwood, M. (ed.) (1994) *Hospital Discharge Workbook: A Manual on Hospital Discharge Practice* (London: Department of Health)

Hindle, D. and Yazbeck, A. (2005) 'Clinical Pathways in 17 European Union Countries: A Purposive Survey', *Australian Health Review*, 29 (1): pp. 94–104

HM Government (2007) *Putting People First: A Shared Vision and Commitment to the Transformation of Adult Social Care* (London: HM Government)

HM Government (2009) *Shaping the Future of Care Together* (London: TSO)

HM Government (2010a) *Recognised, Valued and Supported: Next Steps for the Carers Strategy* (London: Department of Health)

HM Government (2010b) *Healthy Lives, Healthy People* (London: TSO)

Hoggett, P. (2006) 'Conflict, Ambivalence, and the Contested Purpose of Public Organizations', *Human Relations*, 59: pp. 175–194

Holzhausen, E. (2001) *'You Can Take Him Home Now': Carers' Experiences of Hospital Discharge* (London: Carers National Association)

Hudson, B. (2002a) 'Ten Reasons Not to Trust Care Trusts', *Managing Community Care*, 10 (2): pp. 3–11.

Hudson, B. (2002b) 'Integrated Care and Structural Change in England: The Case of Care Trusts', *Policy Studies*, 23 (2), pp. 77–95

Hudson, B. (2004) 'Care Trusts: A Sceptical View' in J. Glasby and E. Peck (eds), *Care Trusts: Partnership Working in Action* (Abingdon: Radcliffe Medical Press)

Hudson, B. (2007) 'What Lies Ahead for Partnership Working? Collaborative Contexts and Policy Tensions?' *Journal of Integrated Care*, 15 (3): pp. 29–36

Hudson, B. (2010) 'Integrated Commissioning: New Context, New Dilemmas, New Solutions?' *Journal of Integrated Care*, 18: pp. 11–19

Humphries, R. *et al.* (2012) *Health and Wellbeing Boards: System Leaders or Talking Shops?* (London: King's Fund)

Hunter, D. (ed.) (2008) *Perspectives on Joint Directors of Public Health Appointments* (London: IDEA)

Hunter, D.J. (2003) *Public Health Policy* (Cambridge: Polity)

Hunter, D.J., Marks, L. and Smith, K.E. (2010) *The Public Health System in England* (Bristol: The Policy Press)

Hunter, D. *et al.* (2011) *Partnership Working and the Implications for govern-ance: Issues Affecting Public Health Partnerships* (Southampton: NHS SDO programme)

Hunter, P. (2009) *Social Enterprise for Public Service: How Does the Third Sector Deliver?* (London: The Smith Institute)

Huxham, C. and Vangen, S. (2005) *Managing to Collaborate: The Theory and Practice of Collaborative Advantage* (Abingdon: Routledge)

Imison, C. (2011) *Reconfiguring Hospital Services* (London: King's Fund)

Jackson, A. (ed.) (2011) *The Councillor's Guide, 2010–2011* (London: Local Government Group)

Jeffrey, C. (2007) 'The Unfinished Business of Devolution', *Public Policy and Administration*, 22 (1): pp. 92–108

Jelphs, K. and Dickinson, H. (2008) *Working in Teams* (Bristol: The Policy Press)

Jordan, J. *et al.* (1998) Whose Priorities? Listening to Users and the Public', *British Medical Journal*, 316: pp. 1668–1670 (30 May).

Kanter, R.M. (1989) *When Giants Learn to Dance* (New York: Simon & Schuster).

Keen, J. and Denby, T. (2009) 'Partnerships in the Digital Age' in J. Glasby and H. Dickinson (eds), *International Perspectives on Health and Social Care: Partnership Working in Action* (Oxford: Wiley-Blackwell)

Kellett, M. (2011) *Children's Perspectives on Integrated Services* (Basingstoke: Palgrave Macmillan)

Kendall, J. (2003) *The Voluntary Sector: Comparative Perspectives in the UK* (London: Routledge)

Kharicha, K. *et al.* (2005) 'Tearing down the Berlin Wall: Social Workers' Perspectives on Joint Working with General Practice', *Family Practice*, 22: pp. 399–405

Kinsman, L. *et al.* (2010) 'What Is a Clinical Pathway? Development of a Definition to Inform the Debate', *BMC Medicine*, 8: p. 31.

Kramer, R.M. and Tyler, T.R. (1995) *Trust in Organizations: Frontiers of Theory and Research* (Thousand Oaks: Sage)

Laming, H. (2003) *The Victoria Climbié Inquiry* (London: HMSO)

Laming, H. (2009) *The Protection of Children in England: A Progress Report* (London: TSO)

Langlands, A. (2003) *Synchronising Higher Education and the NHS* (London: TSO/The Nuffield Trust)

Law Commission (2011) *Adult Social Care* (London: TSO)

Leathard, A. (ed.) (1994) *Going Inter-professional: Working together for Health and Welfare* (Hove: Routledge)

Leathard, A. (ed.) (2003) *Interprofessional Collaboration: From Policy to Prac-tice in Health and Social Care* (Hove: Routledge)

Le Grand, J. (2007) *The Other Invisible Hand: Delivering Public Services through Choice and Competition* (Princeton (NJ): Princeton University Press)

Le Grand, J. and Bartlett, W. (1993) *Quasi-Markets and Social Policy* (Basingstoke: Macmillan)

Le Grand, J., Mays, N. and Mulligan, J.A. (eds) (1998) *Learning from the NHS Internal Market: A Review of the Evidence* (London: Kings Fund)

Leutz, W. (1999) 'Five Laws for Integrating Medical and Social Services: Lessons from the United States and the United Kingdom', *Milbank Memorial Fund Quarterly*, 77: pp. 77–110

Levine, S. and White, P.E. (1962) 'Exchange as a Conceptual Framework for the Study of Interorganizational Relationships', *Administrative Science Quarterly*, 5: pp. 583–601

Lewicki, R.J. and Bunker, B.B. (1995) 'Developing and Maintaining Trust in Work Relationships' in R.M. Kramer and T.R. Tyler (eds), *Trust in Organizations: Frontiers of Theory and Research* (Thousand Oaks: Sage)

Ling, T. (2000) 'Unpacking Partnership: The Case of Health' in J. Clarke and S. Gewirtz (eds), *New Managerialism, New Welfare?* (London: Sage)

Lowndes, V. and Skelcher, C. (1998) 'The Dynamics of Multi-organizational Partnerships: An Analysis of Changing Modes of Governance', *Public Administration*, 76: pp. 313–333

Lukes, S. (1974) *Power: A Radical View* (Basingstoke: Palgrave Macmillan)

Lymberry, M. (2005) *Social Work with Older People: Context, Policy and Practice* (London: Sage)

Lynn, L., Heinrich, C. and Hill, C. (2001) *Improving Governance: A New Logic for Empirical Research* (Washington DC: Georgetown University Press)

Mackintosh, M. (1992) 'Partnerships: Issues of Policy and Negotiation', *Local Economy*, 7: pp. 210–224

Mandelstam, M. (2008) *Community Care Practice and the Law*. 4th edn (London: Jessica Kingsley)

Mannion, R. (2011) 'General Practitioner-led Commissioning in the NHS: Progress, Prospects and Pitfalls', *British Medical Bulletin*, 97 (11): pp. 7–15

Mansfield, H. (1982) 'Accountability and Congressional Oversight' in B. Smith and J. Carroll (eds), *Improving the Accountability and Performance of Government* (Washington: The Brookings Institution)

Manthorpe, J. *et al.* (2010) 'Individual Budgets and Adult Safeguarding: Parallel or Converging Tracks? Further Findings from the Evaluation of the Individual Budget Pilots', *Journal of Social Work*, 11 (4): pp. 422–438

Marks, L. and Hunter, D. (2007) *Social Enterprises and the NHS: Changing Patterns of Ownership and Accountability* (London: UNISON)

Marks, M.L. and Mirvis, P.H. (2001) 'Making Mergers and Acquisitions Work: Strategic and Psychological Preparation', *Academy of Management Executive*, 15: pp. 80–94

Mauger, S. *et al.* (2010) *Involving Users in Commissioning Local Services* (York: Joseph Rowntree Foundation)

Mays, N., Dixon, A. and Jones, L. (2011) *Understanding New Labour's Market Reforms of the English NHS* (London: King's Fund)

McClenahan, J. and Howard, L. (1999) *Healthy Ever After? Supporting Staff through Merger and Beyond* (Abingdon: Health Education Authority)

McCoy, D. *et al.* (2007) 'Carrot and Sticks? The Community Care Act (2003) and the Effect of Financial Incentives on Delays in Discharge from Hospitals in England', *Journal of Public Health*, 29: pp. 281–287.

McDonald, A. (2006) *Understanding Community Care: A Guide for Social Workers. 2nd edn* (Basingstoke: Palgrave Macmillan)

Means, R., Richards, S. and Smith, R. (2008) *Community Care: Policy and Practice*. 4th edn (Basingstoke: Palgrave Macmillan)

Means, R. and Smith, R. (1998) *Community Care: Policy and Practice*. 2nd edn (Basingstoke: Macmillan)

Mencap (2007) *Death by Indifference* (London: Mencap)

Mental Health Network (2011) *Key Facts and Trends in Mental Health* (London: NHS Confederation)

Meyerson, D. and Martin, J. (1987) 'Cultural Change: An Integration of Three Different Views', *Journal of Management Studies*, 24: pp. 623–643

Michael, J. (2008) *Healthcare for All* (London: Independent Inquiry into Access to Healthcare for People with Learning Disabilities)

Miller, R., Dickinson, H. and Glasby, J. (2011) *The Vanguard of Integration or a Lost Tribe? Care Trusts Ten Years On* (Birmingham, Health Services Management Centre)

Milner, J. and O'Bryne, P. (2009) *Assessment in Social Work*. 3rd edn (Basingstoke: Palgrave Macmillan)

Mueller, F., Proctor, S. and Buchanan, D. (2000) 'Team Working in Its Context(s): Antecedents, Nature and Dimensions', *Human Relations*, 3: pp. 1387–1424

National Audit Office (2012) *Healthcare across the UK: A Comparison of the NHS in England, Scotland, Wales and Northern Ireland* (London: TSO)

Needham, C. and Carr, S. (2009) *Co-production: An Emerging Evidence Base for Social Care Transformation* (London: Social Care Institute for Excellence)

Needham, C. (2011) *Personalising Public Services: Understanding the Person-alisation Narrative* (Bristol: The Policy Press)

Neill, J. and Williams, J. (1992) *Leaving Hospital: Older People and Their Discharge to Community Care* (London: HMSO)

New Economics Foundation (2008) *Co-production: A Manifesto for Growing the Core Economy* (London: New Economics Foundation)

Newman, J. (2001) *Modernising Governance: New Labour, Policy and Society* (London: Sage)

NHS (2011) *Developing the NHS Commissioning Board* (London: NHS)

NHS Confederation (2002) *Clinical Networks* (London: NHS Confederation)

NHS Confederation and partners (2011) *Operating Principles for Health and Well-Being Boards: Laying the Foundations for Healthier Places* (London: NHS Confederation)

NHS Future Forum (2012) *Integration– a Report from the NHS Future Forum* (London: NHS Future Forum)

NHS Specialised Services (2010) *Safe and Sustainable: A New Vision for Children's Congenital Heart Services in England – Consultation Document* (London: NHS Specialised Services)

Nicholas, E., Qureshi, H. and Bamford, C. (2003) *Outcomes into Practice: Focusing Practice and Information on the Outcomes People Value* (York: York Publishing Services)

Nolan, M., Grant, G. and Keady, J. (1996) *Understanding Family Care: A Multidimensional Model of Care and Coping* (Buckingham: Open University Press)

Nolan, M. *et al.* (eds) (2003) *Partnerships in Family Care: Understanding the Caregiving Career* (Maidenhead: Open University Press)

Nolte, E., Knai, C. and McKee, M. (2008) *Managing Chronic Conditions: Experience in Eight Countries*, Observatory Studies Series No. 15 (Copenhagen: World Health Organization, European Observatory on Health Systems and Policies)

Office for Public Management (OPM) (2001a) *The Joint Appointments Guide: A Guide to Setting Up, Managing and Maintaining Joint Appointments for Health Improvement between Health Organisations and Local Government* (London: OPM)

Office for Public Management (OPM) (2001b) *Joint Appointments: Case Studies Report* (London, OPM)

Office for Public Management (OPM) (2004) *The Joint Appointments Guide: A Guide to Setting Up, Managing and Maintaining Joint Appointments between Health Organisations and Local Government in Scotland* (London: OPM)

O'Leary, R., Gerard, C. and Bingham, L.B. (2006) 'Introduction to the Symposium on Collaborative Public Management', *Public Administration Review*, 66: pp. 6–9

Oliver, M. (1990) *The Politics of Disablement* (Basingstoke: Macmillan)

Oliver, M. (2009) *Understanding Disability: From Theory to Practice*. 2nd edn (Basingstoke: Palgrave Macmillan)

Oliver, M. and Barnes, C. (1998) *Disabled People and Social Policy: From Exclusion to Inclusion* (Harlow: Longman)

Oliver, M. and Sapey, B. (2006) *Social Work with Disabled People*. 3rd edn (Basingstoke: Palgrave Macmillan)

O'Toole, L.J. and Meier, K.J. (2004) 'Desperately Seeking Selznick: Cooptation and the Dark Side of Public Management in Networks', *Public Administration Review*, 64: pp. 681–693

Ouchi, W. and Johnson, A. (1978) 'Types of Organisational Control and Their Relationship to Organisational Well-Being', *Administrative Science Quarterly*, 23: pp. 292–317

Parker, H. (2006) *Making the Shift: A Review of NHS Experience* (Birmingham: Health Services Management Centre/NHS Institute)

Parker, H. (2009) *Evidence for Transforming Community Services: Services for Long-Term Conditions* (Birmingham: Health Services Management Centre (on behalf of the DH))

Parker, H. and Glasby, J. (2008a) 'Transforming Community Health Services: English Lessons on Not Relying on Organisational Reform', *Health and Social Care in the Community*, 16 (5): pp. 449–450

Parker, H. and Glasby, J. (2008b) 'The Art of the Possible: Reforming Community Health Services', *British Journal of Community Nursing*, 13 (10): pp. 480–486

Parker, M. (2000) *Organisational Culture and Identity* (London: Sage)

Pawson, R. and Tilley, N. (1997) *Realistic Evaluation* (London: Sage)

Payne, M. (2005a) *The Origins of Social Work: Continuity and Change* (Basingstoke: Palgrave Macmillan)

Payne, M. (2005b) *Modern Social Work Theory* (Basingstoke: Palgrave Macmillan)

Payne, M. (2006) *What Is Professional Social Work?* 2nd edn (Bristol: The Policy Press)

Peck, E. and Dickinson, H. (2008) *Managing and Leading in Inter-agency Settings* (Bristol: The Policy Press)

Peck, E. and Dickinson, H. (2009) 'Partnership Working and Organisational Culture' in J. Glasby and H. Dickinson (eds), *International Perspectives on Health and Social Care: Partnership Working in Action* (Oxford: Wiley-Blackwell)

Peck E., Gulliver, P. and Towell, D. (2002) *Modernising Partnerships: An Evaluation of Somerset's Innovations in the Commissioning and Organisation of Mental Health Services* (London: IAHSP King's College)

Peck, E. *et al.* (2004) 'Why Do We Keep Meeting Like This? The Board as Ritual in Health and Social Care', *Health Services Management Research*, 17: pp. 100–109

Peckham, S. and Exworthy, M. (2003) *Primary Care in the UK* (Basingstoke: Palgrave Macmillan)

Pendleton, D. and King, J. (2002) 'Values and Leadership', *British Medical Journal*, 325 (7 Dec.): pp. 1325–1355

Petch, A. (2008a) *Health and Social Care: Establishing a Joint Future?* (Edinburgh: Dunedin Academic Press)

Petch, A. (2008b) 'Safety Matters: The Role of Partnership Working in Safeguarding Adults', *Journal of Integrated Care*, 16 (6): pp. 29–40

Pierre, J. and Peters, B.G. (2000) *Governance, Politics and the State* (New York: St Martin's Press)

Pollock, A. (2005) *NHS PLC: The Privatisation of Our Health Care.* 2nd edn (London: Verso)

Powell Davies, G., Dennis, C. and Walker, C. (2009) 'Self-management with Others: The Role of Partnerships in Supporting Self-Management for People with Long-Term Conditions' in J. Glasby and H. Dickinson (eds), *International Perspectives on Health and Social Care* (Oxford: Blackwell-Wiley)

Prime Minister's Strategy Unit (2005) *Improving the Life Chances of Disabled People* (London: Prime Minister's Strategy Unit)

Pye, A. (2005) 'Leadership and Organizing: Sensemaking in Action', *Leadership*, 1: pp. 31–50

Realpe, A. and Wallace, L.M. (2010) *What Is Co-production?* (London: The Health Foundation)

Reilly, S. *et al.* (2007) 'Care Management in Mental Health Services in England and Northern Ireland: Do Integrated Organisations Promote Integrated Practice?' *Journal of Health Services Research and Policy*, 12: pp. 236–241

Richards, J. (2000) *The Northern Ireland Model – Unifying Health and Social Services: What Care Be Read Across?* (Belfast: QMW Public Policy Seminar

Richardson, S. and Asthana, S. (2005a) 'Policy and Legal Influences on Inter-Organisational Information Sharing in Health and Social Care Services', *Journal of Integrated Care*, 13 (3): pp. 3–10.

Richardson, S. and Asthana, S. (2006b) 'Inter-agency Information Sharing in Health and Social Care Services: The Role of Professional Culture', *British Journal of Social Work*, 36: pp. 657–669

Rogers, A. and Pilgrim, D. (2001) *Mental Health Policy in Britain.* 2nd edn (Basingstoke: Palgrave Macmillan)

Ross, F. and Tissier, J. (1997) 'The Care Management Interface with General Practice: A Case Study', *Health and Social Care in the Community*, 5: pp. 153–61

Rossi, P.H. and Freeman, H.E. (1985) *Evaluation: A Systematic Approach* (Newbury Park, CA: Sage)

Royal Commission on Long Term Care (1999) *With Respect to Old Age: Long Term Care – Rights and Responsibilities* (London: TSO)

Rummery, K. and Glendinning, C. (2000) *Primary Care and Social Services* (Abingdon: Radcliffe Medical Press)

Scottish Executive (2000) *Community Care: A Joint Future* (Edinburgh: Scottish Executive)

Scottish Executive (2001) *Scottish Executive's Response to the Report of the Joint Future Group* (Edinburgh: Scottish Executive)

Scottish Office (1998) *Modernising Community Care: An Action Plan* (Edinburgh: TSO)

Scriven, M. (1991) *Evaluation Thesaurus* (Newbury Park, CA: Sage)

Secretary of State for Health (2012) *Reforming the Law for Adult Care and Support: The Government's Response to the Law Commission Report 326 on Adult Social Care* (London: TSO)

Shapiro, S.P. (1987) 'The Social Control of Impersonal Trust', *American Journal of Sociology*, 93: pp. 623–658

Singh, D. (2006) *Making the Shift: Key Success Factors – A Rapid Review of Best Practice in Shifting Hospital Care into the Community* (Birmingham: Health Services Management Centre/NHS Institute)

Singh, D. and Ham, C. (2005) *Transforming Chronic Care: Evidence about Improving Care for People with Long-Term Conditions* (Birmingham: Health Services Management Centre)

Sitkin, S.B. and Roth, N.L. (1993) 'Explaining the Limited Effectiveness of Legalistic "Remedies" for Trust-Distrust', *Organization Science*, 4: pp. 367–392

Skelcher, C., Mathur, N. and Smith, M. (2004) *Effective Partnership and Good Governance: Lessons for Policy and Practice* (Birmingham: Institute of Local Government Studies, University of Birmingham)

Skills for Care (2010) *The State of the Adult Social Care Workforce in England, 2010* (London: Skills for Care)

Smith, J. et al. (2004) *A Review of the Effectiveness of Primary-Care Led Commissioning and Its Place in the UK NHS* (London: Health Foundation)

Smith, J. and Goodwin, N. (2006) *Towards Managed Primary Care: The Role and Experience of Primary Care Organizations* (Aldershot: Ashgate)

Smith, P. (1996) *Measuring Outcome in the Public Sector* (London: Taylor and Francis)

Social Care Institute for Excellence (2008) *Seldom Heard: Developing Inclusive Participation in Social Care* (London: SCIE)

Social Enterprise Coalition (2009) *State of Social Enterprise Survey, 2009* (London: Social Enterprise Coalition)

Social Work Taskforce (2009) *Building a Safe, Confident Future – The Final Report of the Social Work Task Force* (London: Social Work Taskforce)

Stevens, A. and Gillam, S. (1998) 'Needs Assessment: From Theory to Practice', *British Medical Journal*, 316 (9 May): pp. 1448–1452

Stewart, A., Petch, A. and Curtice, L. (2003) 'Towards Integrated Working across Health and Social Care in Scotland: From Maze to Matrix', *Journal of Interprofessional Care*, 17 (4), pp. 335–50

Stoker, G. and Wilson, D. (2004) *British Local Government into the 21st Century* (Basingstoke: Palgrave Macmillan)

Sullivan, H. and Skelcher, C. (2002) *Working across Boundaries: Collaboration in Public Services* (Basingstoke: Palgrave Macmillan)

Taylor, B. (2011) 'Developing an Integrated Assessment Tool for the Health and Social Care of Older People', *British Journal of Social Work*, 42 (7): pp. 1293–1314

Teasdale, S. (2009) *The Contradictory Faces of Social Enterprise: Impression Management as (Social) Entrepreneurial Behaviour* (Birmingham: Third Sector Research Centre)

Tetenbaum, T.J. (1999) 'Beating the Odds of Merger and Acquisition Failure: Seven Key Practices That Improve the Chance for Expected Integration Synergies', *Organisational Dynamics*, Autumn: pp. 22–36.

Tew, J. (ed.) (2005) *Social Perspectives in Mental Health* (London: Jessica Kingsley)

Timmins, N. (2012) *Never Again? The Story of the Health and Social Care Act 2012* (London: King's Fund)

UPIAS (Union of the Physically Impaired against Segregation) (1976) *Fundamental Principles of Disability* (London: UPIAS)

Vaughan, B. and Lathlean, B. (1999) *Intermediate Care: Models in Practice* (London: King's Fund)

Wade, S. (ed.) (2003) *Intermediate Care of Older People* (London: Whurr Publications)

Waine, B. *et al.* (2005) *Developing Social Care: Values and Principles* (London: Social Care Institute for Excellence)

Wanless, D. (2006) *Securing Good Care for Older People: Taking a Long-Term View* (London: King's Fund)

Weber, M. (1968) *Economy and Society*. Original edition, 1925 (New York: Bedminister Press)

Welsh Assembly Government (2004) *Making the Connections: Delivering Better Services for Wales* (Cardiff: Welsh Assembly Government)

Welsh Assembly Government (2005) *Designed for Life: Creating World Class Health and Social Care for Wales in the 21st century* (Cardiff: Welsh Assembly Government)

Welsh Assembly Government (2006) *Beyond Boundaries: Citizen-Centred Local Services for Wales* (Cardiff: Welsh Assembly Government)

West, M. (2012) *Effective Teamwork: Practical Lessons from Organisational Research.* 3rd edn (Oxford: Blackwell Publishing)

West, M., Borrill, C. and Unsworth, K. (1998) 'Team Effectiveness in Organizations', in C.L. Cooper and I.T. Robinson (eds), *International Review of Industrial and Organizational Psychology Vol. 13* (Chichester: Wiley)

West, M. and Markiewicz, L. (2004) *Building Team-based Working: A Practical Guide to Organizational Transformation* (Oxford: British Psychological Society/Blackwell Publishing)

West, M. *et al.* (2012) *Effectiveness of Multi-Professional Team Working in Mental Health Care* (Birmingham: Aston University)

Wilkinson, J.R. and Murray, S.A. (1998) 'Assessment in Primary Care: Practical Issues and Possible Approaches', *British Medical Journal, 316* (16 May): p. 1524

Williams, V. (2012) *Learning Disability Policy and Practice: Changing Lives?* (Basingstoke: Palgrave Macmillan)

Williams, I., Robinson, S. and Dickinson, H. (2011) *Rationing in Health Care: The Theory and Practice of Priority Setting* (Bristol: The Policy Press)

Williams, R. and Wright, J. (1998) 'Epidemiological Issues in Health Needs Assessment', *British Medical Journal, 316* (2 May): pp. 1379–1382

Williamson, O.E. (1975) *Markets and Hierarchies: Analysis and Antitrust Implications* (New York: Free Press)

Wilson, D. and Game, C. (2006) *Local Government in the United Kingdom.* 4th edn (Basingstoke: Palgrave Macmillan)

Winslow, C. E. (1920) 'The Untilled Fields of Public Health, *Science*, pp. 51, 23

Wistow, G. (2011) *Integration This Time? Liberating the NHS and the Role of Local Government* (London: Local Government Association)

Wistow, G. and Waddington, E. (2006) 'Learning from Doing: Implications of the Barking and Dagenham Experiences for Integrating Health and Social Care', *Journal of Integrated Care*, 14: pp. 8–18.

Wright, J., Williams, R. and Wilkinson, J.R. (1998) 'Development and Importance of Health Needs Assessment', *British Medical Journal* 316 (25 April): pp. 1310–1313

Young, R. *et al.* (2003) *Partnership Working: A Study of NHS and Local Authority Services in Wales* (Manchester/Leeds: Manchester Centre for Healthcare Management/Nuffield Institute for Health)

Zaleznik, A. (1992) 'Managers and Leaders: Are They Different?' *Harvard Business Review*, 3: pp. 126–138

index